W9-CFB-057

PRAISE FOR
HOW TO ARGUE SO YOUR SPOUSE WILL LISTEN

"So many of our reactions are wired into our unhealthy beliefs, and we hurt the ones we love without meaning to. For years Dr. Sharon Morris May has offered couples a safe way to argue that moves them toward intimacy instead of isolation and loneliness. In *How to Argue So Your Spouse Will Listen* she gives us the reason why we argue and how to break the destructive cycle. You'll find great insights and lots of practical help for the day-to-day communications with your mate. If you're married, you need this book!"

— **Dr. Gary Smalley**
Speaker and Author, *I Promise*

"If you're married and you never argue, you don't need this book. You need a book on denial. For everyone else, Dr. Morris May is recommended reading."

— **John Ortberg**
Pastor and Author, Menlo Park
Presbyterian Church

"Without a doubt, *How to Argue So Your Spouse Will Listen* is by far the best book on the topic of marital discord I have ever come across. Dr. Sharon Morris May (who also happens to be my daughter) has excelled at opening up a whole new way of viewing our marital disagreements. Just like those time-lapse movies that depict the beautiful unfolding of a gorgeous bouquet of flowers, this book unfolds the benefits of healthy arguments. It presents a positive perspective on what otherwise can devastate marriages and offers very effective tools that couples can easily apply. This book, unlike any other I have encountered, offers hope to the most troubled of marriages."

— **Archibald D. Hart, PhD, FPPR**
Senior Professor of Psychology
and Dean Emeritus, Graduate
School of Psychology, Fuller
Theological Seminary; and Author,
Thrilled to Death

HOW TO ARGUE SO YOUR SPOUSE WILL LISTEN

6 Principles for Turning Arguments Into Conversations

Sharon Morris May, Ph.D.

THOMAS NELSON
Since 1798

NASHVILLE   DALLAS   MEXICO CITY   RIO DE JANEIRO   BEIJING

© 2007 Sharon Morris May, Ph.D.

All rights reserved. No portion of this book may be reproduced, stored in a retrieval system, or transmitted in any form or by any means—electronic, mechanical, photocopy, recording, scanning, or any other—except for brief quotations in critical reviews or articles, without the prior written permission of the publisher.

Published in Nashville, Tennessee, by Thomas Nelson. Thomas Nelson is a trademark of Thomas Nelson, Inc.

Thomas Nelson, Inc. titles may be purchased in bulk for educational, business, fund-raising, or sales promotional use. For information, please e-mail SpecialMarkets@ThomasNelson.com.

Scripture taken from the NEW CENTURY VERSION®. © 2005 by Thomas Nelson, Inc. Used by permission. All rights reserved.

Library of Congress Cataloging-in-Publication Data

Morris May, Sharon.
    How to argue so your spouse will listen / Sharon Morris May.
       p. cm.
    Includes bibliographical references (p. 209–210).
    ISBN 978-0-8499-1868-1 (pbk.)
      1. Marriage—Religious aspects—Christianity. 2. Interpersonal conflict—Religious aspects—Christianity. 3. Anger—Religious aspects—Christianity. 4. Listening—Religious aspects—Christianity. I. Title.
    BV835.M685 2007   2007023472
    646.7'8—dc22

Printed in the United States of America

07 08 09 10 11 RRD 5 4 3 2 1

To my best friend and gorgeous husband, Mike. Thank you for always being excited about my adventures. You have added to my life in amazing ways. I am glad we are going through life together. I love you.

Matt, Vincent, Alan, and Mitch,
I am proud to call you my sons.

"This is my prayer for [each of us]: that [our] love will grow more and more; that [we] will have knowledge and understanding with [our] love" (Phil. 1:9 NCV).

CONTENTS

INTRODUCTION WHAT IS THIS BOOK BASED ON?

I AM GLAD YOU FOUND YOUR WAY TO THIS BOOK. IT IS MY hope to introduce to you a new and very effective way of making sense of the way you and your spouse argue. Since the way you argue has such a big impact on your marriage, changing how you argue will change your marriage. It will move you from hurt and disconnection to a safe haven marriage. Have hope. It is possible to argue in a way that you and your spouse can hear, understand, and value each other. But before getting into the content of learning how to argue so your spouse will listen, I'd like to share a little background of how this book came about and how I have seen the transforming outcomes these principles can have on a marriage.

How to Argue So Your Spouse Will Listen is based on the work I have conducted in the Haven of Safety Marriage Intensives and Conferences, which help couples make sense of and change the way they argue in order to have an emotionally connected relationship. Couples from all over the country spend two to four days at the Haven of Safety Marriage Intensives for the purpose of growing and healing their marriage. As a result, I have come to be known as a *fight expert*, not because I'm good at arguing with my husband but because as a marriage consultant I sit day in and day out with couples who are stuck arguing. At the intensives and conferences, thousands of husbands and wives have learned the marriage-changing concepts you'll find in this book.

The Haven of Safety Relationship Intensives and Conferences and this book are based on numerous sources. To understand *why* we love and hurt in our relationships, I draw from Attachment Theory, neurobiology of relationships, and Christian principles. To understand *how* couples argue, I draw from research done by psychologist John Gottman and other great observers of marriage relationships. I incorporate principles from Emotionally Focused Therapy (EFT)[1] to understand how to *unravel* arguments and heal the hurts that have accumulated.

Research has shown EFT to be highly effective with couples. Where marriage counseling helps only 35 to 50 percent of couples, EFT has a 70 to 75 percent success rate of helping couples change the way they argue and foster an emotionally connected relationship.[2] These changes do not fade after a few months, which typically happens after other kinds of couple therapy. Four years after counseling with EFT, couples report lasting changes. Further research shows that 90 percent of all couples who go through EFT counseling report *meaningful* changes.

Most important, my work is sifted through Christian principles about life and relationships. My life and clinical work have been profoundly shaped and impacted by my personal relationship with Jesus Christ. Whenever I sit in the room with a couple, I am fully aware of the work God wants to do in husbands and wives and through me as their counselor. Although based on clinical work and reliable research, my Haven of Safety Relationship model is firmly rooted in the fact that we are created by God to be in relationship with Him and others. And for that purpose, God has created within us a relationship system that, when understood, gives insight and clarity to how we connect, why we are hurt by each other, and how we ought to love one another.

Hundreds of couples have shared their stories with me, yet none of the stories in this book are based on any one particular couple. Rather, the stories and conversations are summaries of stories, themes, and issues that I, and other marriage researchers, have found to be common to couples. If you find a story that is similar to yours, then know you are not alone.

I hope this book will give you a new and different way of understanding your arguments as you journey to foster a safe haven with your spouse. Feel free to e-mail me; I look forward to hearing how this book has helped you argue so your spouse will listen.

To the many people in my life who have taught me and encouraged me along the way, I say thank you. I am very appreciative to Debbie Wickwire at Thomas Nelson for believing in this project. I thank editor Laura Kendall for helping me make this book easier to read. To my sister, Sylvia Hart Frejd, thank you for encouraging me in my dreams. And finally, I could not have written this book without the wisdom, encouragement, and incredible editing support of my sister Dr. Catherine Hart Weber. Thank you, sisters; there is strength in teamwork.

—Sharon

I pray that Christ will live in your hearts by faith and that your life will be strong in love and be built on love.

— EPHESIANS 3:17 (NCV)

PART ONE

Why We Love
and Argue
the Way We Do

ONE SO YOU ARGUE

The Power of a Couple's Arguments

WE HAD ARGUED ALL WEEK. WE BOTH HAD TRIED HARD TO get across how we felt about this particular issue. I felt criticized. He felt blamed. We both defended ourselves. Too focused on our own points of view, neither of us was able to understand the other's perspective. I was sure I was right, and he was just as certain he was. We were stuck on reviewing each other's faults and unable to listen to what the other was really trying to say. We walked away and didn't talk for hours. We were left feeling that the other didn't care.

It was early in our relationship, and as we sat out on the front lawn, exhausted in our failed attempt to rehash the argument and try to find some resolution, I noticed how handsome Mike looked. My angry heart softened as I longed to curl up under his arm. Suddenly the issue didn't seem worth the battle, and options for working it out seemed possible. Sensing my tenderness, Mike's crusty heart cracked and he tenderly reached out for me and pulled me close.

"You know, Sharon," he whispered in his deep voice that still has a way of melting my heart, no matter how upset I am with him, "we are not each other's enemy. I know we don't agree on some things, but I really do love you and care for you. We have got to find a way to get our points across without hurting each other so much."

His words raised a lump in my throat. He was right.

We were arguing in a destructive way that was beginning to destroy the bond that connected us. We were slowly breaking the cord that tied our hearts together. Like all couples, Mike and I longed to be heard, understood, and valued by each other. But the way we argued greatly impacted our understanding and emotional connection. We had to learn how to argue so the other would listen—and how to listen so the other would feel understood.

STUCK ARGUING

It is not too difficult to get caught in the heat of an argument. When couples argue, their hurts feel huge and each feels justified in arguing the way he or she does. A wife feels alone when her husband offers a solution instead of listening to how difficult her day was. When she walks away saying, "Forget it, you are only concerned about your own life," he feels helpless in ever being able to please her.

In an attempt to be heard, couples criticize, blame, and defend themselves. They get stuck in the spin cycle of their arguments, going round and round, resolving nothing. When they try to go back and work it out, they can't because when they do, they get stuck arguing about the argument. Attempting to clarify *who* said *what* only triggers a bigger argument. They are left feeling hurt and that the other does not understand their perspective.

Couples learn quickly to tag certain issues as "hot topics" to stay away from in an effort to avoid an argument. A wife hides the credit card bill to delay the inevitable explosion and perceived scolding, or a husband downplays the attractiveness of the new administrative assistant at the office to avoid triggering his wife's angry reaction. Couples then come to a place where they fear they are so far apart on some issues that there would be no way of coming together. Hurts accumulate. In the midst of the hurt and disconnection, couples wonder if they were meant to be together. Many question, "If we were meant to be together, why do we argue so much?" and "Why does getting along take so much work?"

Yet, most couples truly love each other, enjoy being together, and just want to know how to share life together in the most supportive and peaceful way possible.

As a marriage counselor, researcher, and wife, I have come to learn that at the heart of every argument is the longing to be heard, understood, and loved. But couples get caught in the spin cycle of their arguments. The way they argue, staying in their fight cycles, keeps them stuck and prevents them from hearing and understanding each other. Most couples are unaware of how they argue, what they bring to an argument, why they argue, and what keeps their arguments hot and spinning. Most are only aware of what they argue about and how hurt and hopeless they feel when they can't get their spouse to listen and change. When a couple is able to make sense of their arguments, their marriage is transformed.

I write this book because the heart cry of every husband and wife is to know how to argue so his or her spouse will listen, understand, and respond in a considerate and caring manner.

THE WAY YOU ARGUE

All couples argue. Arguing in and of itself is not dangerous to a marriage. What is dangerous is *how a couple argues*. The way a couple argues has the potential to wound and unravel the cord that ties their hearts together.

The words of Paul when he wrote to the church in Galatia come to mind as relevant for all couples today: "The whole law is made complete in this one command: 'Love your neighbor as you love yourself.' If you go on hurting each other and tearing each other apart, be careful, or you will completely destroy each other" (Gal. 5:14–15 NCV).

Although husbands and wives fall in love and marry in hopes of growing old together, sharing life with another human being not only brings a deep comfort but also can be complicated and difficult. Marriage is a journey of two people intertwining in order to share a meaningful life together. Our divorce rate of 50 percent for first marriages 67 percent for second attempts, and 74 percent for the third strike reflects how hard this journey is. It often requires more than love and a strong attraction. To make marriage work, a couple will need to know how to argue. *How you and your spouse argue and how you turn toward each other* will have a profound impact on all aspects of your marriage and life.

An argument not only can ruin an evening or weekend, but when it goes unresolved, it leaves you in a continuous state of stress that impacts every area of your life. How you argue not only impacts your marital happiness and satisfaction but also determines whether or not you will have a good night's sleep; it will influence your mood when you wake up, your frame of mind at work, your attitude with your kids, your energy level at the end of each day, the dreams you and your spouse share for the future, and your overall outlook on life. Continued conflict in the marriage can devastate your whole life.

Most couples say, "We argue because we are different. We are just too different to live under the same roof. What we thought were two puzzle pieces fitting together are now two mismatched puzzle pieces being forced to fit together."

The fact that you and your spouse are different and argue when those differences arise is not detrimental to your marriage. Your differences aren't as important as is your way of dealing with them. Research shows that most problematic issues within your marriage won't get solved anyway. Almost 70 percent of what you disagree about today will probably be what you and your spouse will disagree about four years from now. That is because your differences are in the areas of personality and lifestyle preferences.[1] What disintegrates a couple's marriage and drains every bit of happiness out of the relationship is the way a couple tries to get each other to understand their perspective and differences.

Making *not* arguing your goal does not work either. Research shows that husbands and wives who do not argue when dating or during the early years of their marriages will end up in divorce. Not arguing is just as destructive as arguing.

THE IMPORTANCE OF EMOTIONAL CONNECTION

Psychology and neuroscience confirm what the Bible has been saying throughout the ages: relationships are of vital importance to our well-being. Research shows that the key to health and happiness in our relationships, whether it be with God, our children, friends, or spouse, is our ability to stay emotionally connected despite our differences, disappointments, frustrations, and the arguments that follow. While arguing is not dangerous to your marriage, staying emotionally disconnected is.

The key to arguing successfully is to remain emotionally connected during and after your arguments. Whether you argue or avoid getting into arguments, or agree on such areas as finances, sex, and division of chores, is not as important as whether or not the cycle you get stuck in when arguing leaves you emotionally connected.

Couples marry in hopes of having an emotionally connected relationship. All couples fight for this connection. Husbands and wives so long and thirst for this kind of relationship that they will do anything for one—bitterly argue and fight and even divorce in hopes of finding one with someone new.

When you are emotionally connected to your spouse, your marriage relationship becomes a safe haven to which you can turn for care, courage, and comfort. Research has shown that when a couple perceives their marriage to be a safe haven, they flourish in life. They are better able to manage the difficult times, are less depressed, do better at work, heal faster from wounds and surgeries, live longer, and live healthier. And so do children from homes that are safe havens. When your marriage is going well, your children do better at school, they recover from stressful situations, they are able to manage their emotions, their wounds heal faster, they are less aggressive with their peers, they have fewer problems adjusting, and they are less likely to divorce once married.

You probably had an idea of this from the seasons when you and your spouse were emotionally connected and doing well. Life was manageable when you knew you could turn to each other to be supported and encouraged when work was stressful. Kids seemed more manageable, or, at least, you were able to deal with the chaos of the house a whole lot better when you were emotionally connected.

When you understand the hurts, emotions, and "dragons" (a term I'll explain later) that fuel your arguments, you are able to recognize the cycles you get stuck in when arguing. You can then prevent your arguments from going sideways, get unstuck from the spin cycle of your arguments, and turn toward each other. You are able to stop criticizing, blaming, or defending yourselves and realize that you both are actually on the same team. You'll learn to say, "Let me start over. I feel very frustrated and think everything I just said sounded very critical." Or you are able to open the door you just slammed shut and go back to your spouse and say, "I love you and care for you and, even though we disagree right now, I don't want to hurt you. Let's try to understand each other instead of blaming each other and defending ourselves."

When you and your spouse are emotionally connected, the bond that ties the two of you together will be secure. Your relationship will become a source of strength and comfort and, as a team, you'll be able to weather any storm of life.

Knowing how to argue in a way that keeps you and your spouse emotionally connected is vitally important to a lasting and satisfying marriage. The purpose of this book is to help you and your spouse on your journey toward arguing so you will be able to listen and understand each other's perspective and respond in ways that keep you emotionally connected, no matter how different you are or how much you might disagree on an issue.

IF WE LOVE EACH OTHER, WHY DO WE ARGUE?

You and your spouse are different. Even if you found your way to each other on any *match-you-up* Web-based dating service, you have discovered that you are different and don't always agree on everything. These differences often become big and trigger emotionally charged arguments.

No one taught you and your spouse how to argue constructively. Sure, there were the debate classes in high school and the speaker-listener techniques you learned at your last marriage conference. But there was no section in your premarital class on how to argue with your spouse so he or she would listen and understand you. Nor were there any questions or practice sessions on the dating service to prepare you to understand what would bug your spouse, trigger his alarms, raise her dragons, and fuel an argument. Like most couples, nothing prepared you for how your spouse would argue and how you would react to what is said in the midst of the argument. These are things you've discovered the hard way during the years of marriage.

There are not many places a couple can go to discover how to argue in more effective ways. Couples don't readily sit around the table in their Sunday school classes sharing how they got caught in their fight cycles just the night before. It is a difficult journey, learning how to argue so your spouse will listen. Many couples navigate it alone, when they don't need to.

SHOULD MARRIAGE BE THIS HARD?

Some myths we need to get over are "Getting along should not take this much work," "Being married should not be this difficult," and "If we disagree this much, then maybe we aren't meant for each other."

Every couple argues. Why? Because we are all individual human beings with our own thoughts, fears, hurts, desires, and ideas of how things should be. We all share our feelings and react to being hurt and disappointed in different ways. Arguing is inevitable where there are two people with two different views.

At one point or another, you and your spouse will try to get your views across to each other. Whether it is what time you think the kids should go to bed, how quickly the trash should be taken out, or whether her mother can stay for one or four weeks after the baby is born, if you and your spouse have different opinions and each feels strongly about them, an argument could start.

As my wise mother, Kathleen, who has been happily married to my father, Archibald Hart, for over fifty years said, "Marriage is hard work!"

Getting along with imperfect human beings is hard work for everyone. If you think about it, we are imperfect human beings attempting to live with another imperfect human being, each bringing into the marriage relationship different strengths, imperfections, selfishness, needs, longings, dreams, and fears. Blending yours with your spouse's is not an easy task. Just as staying in shape is hard work (especially after forty years of age), so is a marriage. When we realize the time, effort, self-control, and commitment it takes to stay in shape, why would we put any less effort into what is most important in our lives: our valued relationship? The reward of putting your energy into fostering a safe haven in which you are seen, heard, understood, and valued is well worth it.

There is a constructive, considerate way to argue and then there is a destructive, destroying way to argue. Learning to break the habit of one and to grow and foster the other is the journey—the journey that awaits you.

To grow your marriage, you will need to take notice of your moment-by-moment interactions with each other. You will need the courage to invest time and energy into your own personal growth as well as change how you talk, relate, and react to each other. Despite all the arguing and hurts between you and your spouse, you will each need to risk forgiving and reconnecting. You will need to deal with your resentment and anger and choose to be considerate, kind, and respectful toward each other again.

Hope for repairing a marriage wounded by years of arguing and accumulated hurt is available to couples who are willing to be intentional and go the extra mile for what is best for their marriage. Nurturing your marriage is a daily, continuous challenge, but the result is a continuous blessing.

HOW TO BEST USE THIS BOOK

To get the most out of this book, read the chapter then complete the questions that follow. Take what you find to be relevant to your life and put it in practice. To make what you learn real and second nature, you will need to lay down new neural pathways. That means when the same old situation arises, you will need to choose a new response or reaction. Old, automatic reactions are stubborn and hard to change because they have become such big parts of your daily way of communicating with your spouse. It won't be easy to change your scolding tone of voice or your automatic reflex to criticize, or learn to just listen empathetically, or risk coming out from the safety of hiding to share your feelings. Neither will it be easy to take a second look at a situation from your spouse's perspective. To have lasting change, you will need to practice and practice the principles until they become the new way of being between you and your spouse.

It is best to read this book together as a couple, but I am aware that you and your spouse might be stuck arguing or too disconnected to do so. If you are reading it without your spouse, then start the journey on your own. God is calling you to grow in who you are.[2] Choose today who you want to become and the type of person you want to be, regardless of how your spouse reacts. If your spouse continues to be defensive whenever you try to point out anything, instead of clicking into your usual nasty reaction as an attempt to protect your heart, try a different way. Try a way that has integrity. You can make a difference in your own experience of your marriage, whether or not your spouse ever reads this book or changes. You will gain insight into your own life, your emotional world, and how your past impacts how you argue today. You will learn constructive ways of expressing your emotions and talking with your spouse about what is important to you. In doing so, you will develop character and grow as a person.

As you begin to look at your relationship through a new lens, you will begin to unravel your arguments, heal your hurts, and find ways to argue more constructively. You'll find ways to talk so your spouse will listen and understand you. And when you hear and understand each other, you will have an emotionally connected marriage, one that will last a lifetime.

QUESTIONS AND EXERCISES

Where are you in your relationship? The following list of statements will help you focus on how you understand your arguments. To gauge how relevant each statement is to you, answer: Hardly at all, Sometimes, or Most of the time.

Hardly at all   **Sometimes**   **Most of the time**

1. Despite all the arguing between my spouse and me, we don't value and care for each other.

2. We are not aware of how our personalities, early growing-up experiences, and fears impact how we argue.

3. Our arguments don't seem to be about the "topic" we are arguing about.

4. Sometimes we react bigger than the situation calls for.

5. It is not my intention to say hurtful things or shut my spouse out, but I do.

6. One of us tries to calm things down while the other feels he or she has to state his or her case stronger and louder to be understood.

7. I often get so mad or frustrated that I forget the good about my spouse when we are arguing.

8. There are some hurtful situations I can't let go of, even though my spouse has apologized for them many times.

9. We disagree on when to come back and discuss and resolve an argument.

10. When we come back and discuss our arguments, another argument often starts, so hardly any of our arguments ever get resolved.

11. We have a very difficult time agreeing on what the other should say when apologizing for his or her part in the argument.

12. It is hard to stay connected, caring, and considerate when we discuss hot topics.

13. Generally, my spouse and I are not good friends, not very connected or loving to each other.

To score: If you answered "Sometimes" or "Most of the time" for any of the above questions, then you need to read on.

TWO WHAT KEEPS US CLOSE
AND CONNECTED

The Inner Workings of Our Relationship System

JACK AND DIANE HAD JUST SENT THEIR LAST CHILD OFF TO college, and on the ride home she felt a little blue. She reached for Jack's hand, to which he responded, "No, I'm all sweaty." Yes, in her mind she remembered how nervous he was when saying good-bye to their daughter, but deep inside she felt so vulnerable. His comment felt rejecting. She really needed a bit of comforting but instead of telling Jack how she was feeling, she folded her arms and silently looked out the window for the rest of the ride. Her longing to be comforted was tangled with her hurt from being rejected.

Jack asked if she was okay. What Diane found coming out was her irritation as she said, "What am I supposed to be? You drive fast, don't want to stop for lunch—what do you expect?" Diane caught herself and thought, *I am a grown woman. I know he loves me, so why am I hurt and feeling so rejected by his not wanting to hold my hand?*

Here is another scenario. For an entire week, Rick's wife, Lauren, came home late from work, bringing with her a folder full of reports to read. Sure, Rick was capable of picking up the slack around the house while she sat over her papers, but he missed his wife. And even though he felt sad and alone, he also felt hurt and angry.

One night as Lauren reminded Rick to take the dog out, he found himself saying, "This house is chaotic, Lauren, because you have not yet learned how to balance your life."

Hearing Rick's criticism, Lauren felt attacked and unsupported. And so she defended herself, telling Rick he was "negative and draining" and that she did not want to talk with him if he was going to criticize her. This was not the response Rick was expecting. He actually wanted Lauren to see how much he missed her and for her to find a bit of time for them to spend together. Rick went silent and withdrew.

CREATED FOR CONNECTION

At times we all wonder why being connected to our spouse is so important. Why does our spouse's attention matter so much? When we miss our husband, why do we feel a mixture of sadness and anger? Why does it feel so uncomfortable, even hurtful, when we feel our wife is not there for us? Why is it a big deal when we feel our spouse is not understanding, considerate, or close?

> "Love the Lord your God with all your heart, all your soul, and all your mind." This is the first and most important command. And the second command is like the first: "Love your neighbor as you love yourself." All the law and the writings of the prophets depend on these two commands.
>
> —Matthew 22:37–40 (NCV)

Basically, it's because God created us that way. We were designed to be in a close and connected relationship with God and others, and the love connection we experience in our most significant relationships means everything to us.

We are at our best when we live connected to God and to those we care about and who care about us. God intended it to be that way. We thrive when we are close and connected with those we love and are anxious and distressed when we are not.

> All of us find security in being with people we know well and are apt to feel anxious and insecure in a crowd of strangers. Particularly in times of crisis or distress do we seek our closest friends and relatives. The need for companionship and the comfort it brings is a very central need in human nature.[1]
>
> —John Bowlby

Because our relationships are so vitally important to our well-being, God created within us a "relationship system." It is also known as our attachment system. Our relationship system has one objective: to help us stay connected with others. And in its efforts to do that, it has an intricate mechanism that causes us to feel powerful emotions and respond in a particular manner when our connection with others is not optimal. It is our relationship system that causes us to yearn for someone to love, connects us to those we like, helps us turn toward our loved one whenever we are sad, mad, or happy, and lets us know when our relationships are not going well.

This system was crucial in our first relationships, teaching us about love and shaping how we related to others. It is also in constant motion in our relationships today, always involved in and impacting how we relate with others and how we love—and argue—with our spouse.

In marriage our relationship system keeps us close and connected to our spouse—and very alert when we are not. It not only keeps you and your spouse connected but it also causes you to react and argue with each other. The intricate system is at work whenever you reach for each other, don't have enough time together, are hurt by each other, or feel disconnected. If you get into an argument, you can be certain that your relationship system was somehow involved.

In this chapter I will explain the key aspects of the relationship system: how it was at work when you were growing up and how it is active in your marriage today. By becoming aware of this system, you will begin to make sense of why you react the way you do when you are hurt or disconnected from your spouse. You will gain insight into why you feel warm and safe when you are close and connected and hurt and upset when you are not. This will help you experience yourself and your spouse in a new way, allowing you to choose different ways of relating and arguing—ways that will draw the two of you together.

IMPACT OF OUR EARLY RELATIONSHIPS

Right from the start of life, our whole being is wired to be in relationship. Our first relationship was with our parents, and it was in this first relationship that we learned about love, life, and the world around us. (I will refer to all early caregivers, whether it was your aunt or uncle, grandparent, foster parent, or stepparent, simply as your parents.) When we were babies we learned how to reach for and give love to another person and how to react when we are hurt. As we grew older, our siblings, relatives, and friends also became significant and influential relationships. And when you married, your spouse became your most important relationship. The bond that joins you and your spouse together is a unique and powerful bond.[2]

While growing up, every interaction we had with our parents and other significant people was vitally important to us and impacted our brains and personal development—shaping our view of life. These experiences were central in shaping who we are and who we became.

> Our brains are structured to be in relationship with other people in a way that shapes how the brain functions and develops. For these reasons, attachment experiences are a central factor in shaping our development.[3]
>
> —Daniel Siegel

The way your parents and loved ones interacted with you, responded to you, nurtured you, and emotionally connected with you laid down the pattern for how you love and react in your marriage today. But before I describe how, let me explain the amazing relationship system that is at work in us and why it is such an integral part of our being.

THE RELATIONSHIP SYSTEM

Did you know that your body has a complex alarm system that alerts you when your connections are not safe, comfortable, or certain? This powerful relationship system allows you to form emotional attachment bonds that keep you tightly connected to your loved ones.[4]

When you were a child, it was your relationship system that kept you connected to your parents and alert to how close or far they were from you. When you first met your spouse, your relationship system kept your interest and attention and helped you fall in love with your spouse-to-be. When you married, your spouse became very important to you, and your relationship system continued, the best way it knows how, to make sure you *stay* connected. And as paradoxical as it sounds, you and your spouse argue and fight to *keep* this connection.

This complex relationship system is not only an emotional but also a *neurobiological system*. Think of it as very similar to your physical pain system. Just as your brain is wired to keep you safe from harm and alerts you through pain when you are hurt or in danger, so does your relationship system alert you—through a very complicated neurobiological pathway—when you are not connected to your loved one.

I will explain the neurobiology of the relationship system and argument in chapter 4. For now, though, it is important to understand that our relationship system is at work in us from the day we are born to the day we die, making sure we are connected safely to those we love. To begin, let me give you a brief overview of this relationship system.

THE INNER WORKINGS OF THE RELATIONSHIP SYSTEM

Your relationship system has four primary functions in your marriage: it helps you keep *close proximity, a safe haven, and a secure base,* and it provides you with a relationship *alarm system.* Each is vitally important in the process of:

- forming a relationship with your spouse,
- keeping your relationship close and connected, and
- attempting to repair your relationship when you are disconnected or when things don't go well.

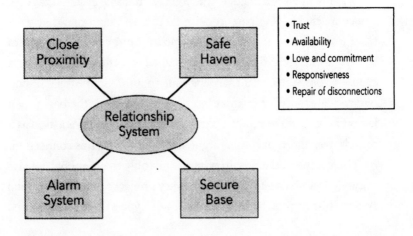

1. Close Proximity

We are naturally drawn to being physically close to our loved one when we are hurt, scared, lonely, and sad as well as when we are happy, excited, or just wanting to share an experience. When we are near the person we love, we feel a sense of peace, security, and contentment. You have seen this at work when a child clings to the skirt of his mother or when a husband reaches for the hand of his wife as they walk down the street. It is our relationship system that keeps us seeking the physical proximity of those we love.

In the early years of our relationships, whether it's with our parents, friends, or other loved ones, spending time together and being close to that person is what initially builds the bond. Babies become familiar with their parents' faces and smells and long for the optimal level of closeness with their parents.

The cord that ties you and your spouse's lives together was first braided during your dating years. When you spent time together you got to know each other, you became more familiar with each other every day, and your hearts and lives began to weave together. Just being together was of high importance as your relationship grew. Now it continues to be natural to want to be close to your spouse, to long for him and miss him when he's gone, and to enjoy him when he's nearby. Of course, how comfortable your parents were with closeness impacts how comfortable you are with closeness in your marriage today. Our early experiences along with our personalities and temperaments impact how we define *closeness* and how comfortable we are with touching and holding our spouse.

2. A Safe Haven

When growing up, your parents became a safe haven to which you could turn for love, safety, and care. As you grew older, you continued to live in the shelter of your most important relationships, and today that safe haven is your marriage.

A safe haven in marriage is like an acacia tree. While growing up in South Africa I saw these restful trees scattered all across the countryside. I'm sure you've seen pictures of their broad branches and flat tops, like large, open umbrellas. Their branches stretch out wide, casting large shadows across the hot ground. In the wild, animals will rest in the shadow of the acacia trees, escaping the heat of the day and finding safety from dangers of the bush. Like the resting shade of the acacia tree found in Africa, you and your spouse become safe havens for each other, where you can come home at the end of each day and experience comfort, understanding, respect, safety, and rest in the shelter of each other.

The image I have of a safe haven is given in Psalm 91. There we are told that safety is ours when we live in the shadow of God: "Those who go to God Most High for safety will be protected by the Almighty. I will say to the LORD, 'You are my place of safety and protection. You are my God and I trust you'" (vv. 1–2). And just as God longs for us to live in His shelter, we were also created to live in the shelter of each other. We are meant to be safe havens where our spouses can find emotional safety, love, and care.

What makes a safe haven marriage? There are five vitally important ingredients.

Trust. A safe haven is fostered when our loved one is dependable, reliable, and emotionally trustworthy. Your trust in others is first shaped in your relationship with your parents. As a child, you trust your parents to be there for you: pick you up after school, protect you from harm, and provide for your needs. You also trust them to be emotionally safe and predictable, not unexpectedly harsh, rejecting, or neglectful. You trust your parents to love and care for you, no matter what.

In your marriage, you need your spouse to be trustworthy and predictable in practical ways, such as paying the bills on time, not overspending, being where they say they will be, and keeping their commitments. But you also long to emotionally trust your spouse with the deep places of your heart—with *you*. When you and your spouse trust each other, you are able to turn toward each other with ease and assurance. You are willing to put your heart into the hand of your spouse because you know she or he has your best interest in mind. We all long to know that despite all our arguing, our spouse loves us and can be trusted with our heart and life.

> We become a safe haven for our spouse when we provide:
> - *trust*
> - *love and commitment*
> - *emotional and physical availability*
> - *responsiveness*
> - *repair of disconnections*

Again, our childhood experiences affect our ability to trust: when growing up, if others were not trustworthy, then you probably have difficulty trusting your spouse to be there for you. The old experience of being let down and disappointed will creep into your interactions.

Love and Commitment. The backbone of marriage is love and commitment, providing the firm and unmovable foundation of permanence. Love assures that your spouse values you, respects you, and chooses you. Commitment assures that your spouse will be there to love, respect, value, and be there for you "for better or worse . . . through sickness and health . . . until death do you part." There is permanence in "we." There is a deep assurance that no matter how difficult the marriage gets, neither person will give up and walk away. Instead, we will both choose to grow, change, and fight *for* the marriage. The *safety* of your safe haven is strengthened when you

have the confidence that you both love each other and both are in
the relationship for life—the way marriage was intended.

Emotional and Physical Availability. Your marriage becomes a safe
haven when you and your spouse are emotionally as well as physically available to each other. You're attuned, sensitive, and emotionally present with each other. But this may be difficult or easy,
depending on how you were raised.

As we grow up, our parents' physical and emotional availability
is crucial for our development. For example, when a father is
attuned to his son, he is able to understand what his son is experiencing and needing and then guide his son in making sense of and
expressing his emotions and needs. He emotionally connects with
his son. Some parents find such emotional connections easy and
enjoyable. But depending upon the experiences your parents had
growing up, this way of relating could have been very unfamiliar or
uncomfortable to them—and now the same may be true for you.

Whether or not your parents were emotionally available and
attuned to you will impact your ability to be attuned to your spouse.
As Jack said, "My parents never asked me, 'What are you feeling?' so
today I have no idea how to be attuned to my wife, never mind
knowing what to do with her emotions."

In marriage, intimacy is fostered when we feel seen and understood by our spouse. When you are emotionally available and attuned
to your spouse, you express care not only through your words but
also through your facial expressions, tone of voice, bodily gestures,
and timing and intensity of your responses. Your spouse can say of
you, "You really do sense what I am feeling; you *get me.*" An incredible
intimacy then connects your hearts, creating a safe haven between
the two of you.

Emotional predictability is also crucial to a couple's sense of security within the marriage. We need to be able to count on our spouse

to be emotionally safe and predictable. Just as children are confused when their parents say they love them but then frequently fly off the handle and lash out in bursts of anger, so; too, is a spouse hurt by a partner's emotional unpredictability. If you can trust your spouse's moods and emotions, you know that he or she will be available and you don't have to walk around on eggshells wondering when something will trigger an angry response or whether they will be irritated at one more question, or go into a sulk for the evening because of something you did.

When the emotional connection in marriage is disrupted, the relationship doesn't feel like a safe haven. But when you and your spouse are able to be physically and emotionally present and connected, you each feel understood and you each can say, "Yeah, you *get* me."

Responsiveness. It is of vital importance to know your spouse will respond to you in an understanding and considerate manner, weighing his or her perspective with your own in the best interest of each other and the relationship. When you and your spouse do this, you foster a safe haven in your marriage.

Responding to each other's perspective lets your spouse know you "considered" him or her and promotes a feeling of "us." And when you respond in a respectful, considerate, and kind manner, each of you feels understood, accepted, cared for, respected, appreciated, and valued.

Now this doesn't mean that you do whatever your spouse wants to keep the peace. Allowing bad behavior, disrespect, rudeness, and irritability is not responding in the best interest of the relationship. You don't sulk to control each other's behavior or yell and criticize in an attempt to get your spouse to listen.

But it does mean that a wife may need to carve out time in the evening to listen as her husband shares about his day. To feel connected, you both need active conversations in which you are each emotionally engaged, sharing personal thoughts and feelings, and responding in a considerate manner. Or it could mean that when a husband hears the kids yelling and knows dinner is not yet done, he will put down his computer game, come into the kitchen, and say, "Hey, need help?" That's responsiveness.

Couples are also creating a safe haven when they maintain a mutual understanding that they won't make decisions (whether it is to spend money, invite the in-laws over, or pick a vacation spot) without considering each other's perspective and keeping each other in mind.

Repairing Disconnections. Crucial to a relationship being a safe haven is a couple's ability to repair the hurts and disconnections in the relationship. In marriage this happens when you are able to turn toward each other, attempt to understand each other, make sense of your arguments, understand why the argument went sideways, heal the hurts inflicted during the argument, and then emotionally reconnect. These *repair efforts* restore the relationship, affirming that you are once again each other's safe haven. Repairing disconnections is the most powerful thing you can do in your marriage. John Gottman's research shows that when a couple is unable to repair their offenses after an argument, they are unable to emotionally connect, and the hurt from living in an emotionally disconnected marriage eventually causes a couple to grow apart. Coming together after an argument is often as simple as reassuring each other: "I know we said harsh words to each other, but despite everything, you mean the world to me. Yes, we disagree, but I still value you." What a sweet safe haven this fosters.

3. A Secure Base

Sometimes we just need to hear the voice of our spouse say, "You can do it; I believe in you," as we nervously walk out the door to give a presentation at work. When your relationship is a safe haven, it becomes a secure base from which you can confidently venture out into the world. Well loved and supported, you are ready to explore and face life's challenges and adventures as a secure person. When you know you are loved and valued and have someone who supports you, you have the inner strength and courage to explore, grow, and become, all the while knowing that you can come home and be loved, valued, and cared for. Life becomes easier to face when you know you have someone who believes in you and will be there for you, no matter what. And . . . well, there is just about anything you can face together.

4. Relationship Alarm System

As we have discovered, the mission of the relationship system is to maintain a sense of security that our loved one will be our safe haven—always trustworthy, committed, available, responsive, and willing to repair hurts and ruptures when we experience them. If we feel that our loved one is close, accessible, and responsive enough, then all is well. Things don't have to be perfect, just good enough.

Whether a child or adult is in a state of security, anxiety, or distress is determined in large part by the accessibility and responsiveness of his principal attachment figure.[5]

—JOHN BOWLBY

Although we were designed for and we long for a safe haven, there are plenty of times when our safe haven doesn't feel so safe. Often it can be the slightest thing that causes us to say, "Hey, you weren't considering me when you said or did that!" Maybe what your husband thinks is good enough isn't good enough for you. Or the way your wife does something, quite frankly, irritates. Or you feel your spouse is not emotionally available and not considering your perspective. Then what happens? That is when the relationship system once again takes a major role.

When we sense that our loved one is not close, emotionally accessible, or responsive, the relationship system *sounds the alarms.* (As you will discover in a later chapter on the neurobiology of an argument, an alarm within your brain is literally triggered, alerting your body that your haven does not feel so safe.) And what follows is certain to trigger an argument.

Our bodies, brains, and emotions are all fully engaged in this complex process of attempting to restore the optimal level of connectedness. If there is an argument, your relationship alarm system had everything to do with getting it started and keeping it fueled. Once you understand the various factors impacting your whole relationship system, you will never be able to argue the same way again. So keep reading.

The Assessment: Are You My Safe Haven? The goal of your relationship system is to make your marriage a safe haven, in which you are meaningfully connected with your spouse. Your relationship system is constantly scanning your relationship—assessing whether or not your spouse is available and responsive—for these essential assurances regarding your spouse:

- Can I trust you will be there for me if I need you?
- Do you love, respect, and care about me?
- Can I trust you to be committed to me and to *us?*
- Will you be emotionally and physically available?
- Will you respond to me in a caring and considerate manner?
- Will you repair our hurts and reconnect when we are disconnected?

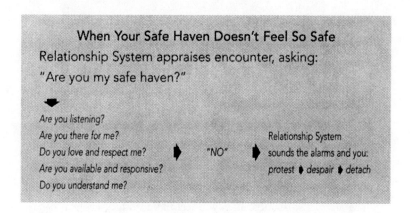

When Your Safe Haven Doesn't Feel So Safe
Relationship System appraises encounter, asking:
"Are you my safe haven?"

Are you listening?
Are you there for me?
Do you love and respect me? ▶ "NO" ▶ Relationship System sounds the alarms and you:
Are you available and responsive? protest ◆ despair ◆ detach
Do you understand me?

If the answer to any of these questions is *no* or *maybe* or *uncertain*, your relationship alarm system is triggered. We respond in a way aimed to get our loved one's attention and restore the relationship. We react in hopes that our spouse will realize the hurtful thing he or she is doing, apologize, and act differently.

Situations That Sound Off the Alarm. Our relationships are so important to us that our relationship system is finely tuned to the slightest changes and nuances in them. A tone of voice, a roll of the eyes, a frown or curled-up lip, an exhale, folded arms, a delay in answering can all trigger the alarm system, signaling that the haven is not so safe.

This alarm system is designed to be triggered and sound off in several different situations, such as:

"I need you!"

When we need the closeness, care, and comfort of our loved one, such as when we are hurt, scared, in need, sad, lonely, happy, joyous, or excited, our attachment system draws us to those we love. Remember, as a child you drew a picture you were proud of and were eager to share it with your mom. As adults, when we hear interesting news at work, we sometimes can't wait to come home and tell our spouse. Or when we are scared at night, we just need to know someone is there.

"Come closer—give me space."

We all have a comfort level regarding closeness. Our alarm sounds off when we sense our loved one is too close or not as close or connected as we would like. This may be when we're feeling alone or when we've felt disconnected from our spouse all week. The alarm also sounds when you feel the need for personal space and time alone—something introverts, who generally prefer to refuel on their own, often feel.

"Ouch! That hurt me!"

What our spouse says or does often hurts. This happens when you feel he or she is untrustworthy, emotionally unavailable, or unresponsive. It hurts when your spouse doesn't keep to the budget as planned or suddenly ends a conversation that is very important to you by abruptly saying, "I am done talking about this." And it hurts when your spouse gives you a look of irritation when you ask for help. Because your spouse means so much to you, these moments hurt.

Emotions That Arise When the Alarm Sounds Off. Because our relationships are of such vital importance to our well-being, our strongest emotions are felt when our alarm system signals that our haven is not safe.[6] When your spouse is not emotionally or physically available to you, the following emotions begin to well up within you.

- Anger: "How dare you ignore me, be unhelpful, not support and take my side, or think my view is wrong."
- Hurt: "Ouch! It hurts when you see me in a negative light, push me away, reject me, are irritated at me, or are not there when I need you."

- Fear: "I doubt that you consider me when you make your decisions. I fear you don't value me or won't be there for me."

- Rejection: "I don't feel valued, desired, or chosen by you. I feel pushed out, ignored, not wanted by you."

- Disrespected: "I don't feel you value what I have to offer or what I contribute to the relationship. You fail to recognize and respect my strengths and qualities."

- Loss: "You shut me out after our argument. I feel alone when you show little interest in my need or hurt."

- Sadness: "I am grieved when you aren't willing to see the situation from my perspective." "I miss you when you pull away or when we are upset with each other." "I feel sad when rejected, disrespected, or not valued by you."

- Frustration: "I want to be connected and not have a wedge between us. But I don't know what to do to get you to understand me and not be so upset with me." "I already told you that when you do those things it hurts me."

HOW WE RESPOND
WHEN THE ALARMS SOUND OFF

We humans have a basic, innate way of responding when we're disconnected from a loved one, specifically a spouse. A sequence of reactions are automatically set in motion, all affected by our individual personalities and earlier relationship experiences. John Bowlby says we follow this natural sequence of reactions:

1. Protest

Most couple's arguments arise out of a spouse's "protest" to the partner's seeming unavailability or insensitivity. The protest is usually filled with anger, hurt, and frustration.

Just as in the first opening story of this chapter with Diane and Jack, Diane's relationship system causes her to reach for Jack when she feels sad. But as she puts her hand out in hopes of its being held, she finds Jack is not physically or emotionally available. His unwillingness to comfort her sounds off her relationship alarm system. Her longing to be connected to Jack is mixed with her angry protests. She is pulled between: "I miss you and want you close . . . but I am angry that you are not there for me."

In the second opening story Lauren and Rick's anger that arose during their argument was an "anger of hope." The anger of hope (a term used by Bowlby) in essence says, "I am angry that you hurt me or were not there for me. But I have hope that if I let you know of my hurt, you will see my hurt, be impacted by it, want to repair it, and work to restore our connection." Rick got angry in *hopes* of his wife seeing his hurt and making efforts to spend time with him.

In most marriages the protests often get louder, more intense, and harsher. A wife often says, "If I don't state my case louder, then he will just keep his own view of the situation and never understand mine." Or a husband keeps repeating his view, like a lawyer, with more assertion, saying, "If my wife could just see the situation from my perspective, then she would not be so upset with me." Couples get stuck in powerful emotional protests, all the while just longing to be seen, heard, and understood.

2. Sadness and despair

After we realize that all the protesting and stating our case louder will not impact our spouse, a sadness and despair follows. Just as in the earlier scenario when Diane needed comfort but ended up sitting quietly, looking out the window and feeling hopeless, despair sets in when you feel that nothing you say will make a difference. You feel nothing will change, and a sadness sets in. Yet, despite all the conflict, you still miss your spouse. Despite all your arguing, you still long to be close and connected.

Rick at first protested Lauren's absence, but he wasn't able to communicate his heart, and the argument ended up going sideways. So instead of a resolution, he grieved the loss of his wife's warmth and companionship. In his heart, Rick knew that he just wanted to be close to and find happiness with Lauren, but his longing, hurt, and frustration all came out as anger and blame.

This experience is typical for many couples. After years of arguing and constantly feeling as though your spouse will never understand you, a long-term sadness and despair can set in. This sadness is what often causes an increase in negative interactions and, ultimately, depression in marriage. That is because a spouse still has an anger of hope—an anger that arises and says, "I still love you, long to be connected to you, but I just don't know what to do with all that has not changed and the unresolved hurt that has accumulated." Despite all the conflict that has gone on, a couple still longs to be connected with each other; they just don't know how.

3. Detachment

After fighting for months, and maybe years, without being able to repair the hurts and disconnections, a couple drifts apart and begins to live separate lives. The husband and wife find their own interests and carve out independent lives for themselves. They have their own friends, hobbies, and routines and only come together to take care of household chores or parenting responsibilities. They begin to close their hearts toward each other as a defensive way of dealing with their hurts and sorrows. Yet underneath their sense of helplessness and disconnection, a seed of hope often remains. "I never wanted to drift apart," Andrew explained to his wife of fourteen years. "I just didn't know how to deal with the negativity between us. All we did was argue. I guess I finally withdrew and started doing things without you. It was less conflictual, less painful that way."

THE LENS THROUGH WHICH YOU VIEW LIFE

While you were growing up, each gesture of caring and emotional response was stored in your memory, informing you how others would be there, or not be there, and how to react in return. These experiences were internalized and became your "internal working models." These models became the patterns for how you respond in relationships today.

Here's how they work: If your parents and loved ones were "there for you" when you were growing up, you internalized the positive assurance of others' love and care, as well as the ease in obtaining it. You feel comfortable giving and receiving comfort and view others as being there for you if you need them. But if you had rejecting experiences growing up, you internalized those experiences, and they became the lens through which you view life, which says, "Don't expect much from your relationships because you will only be rejected." And so you don't readily turn to others for support, but rather become self-sufficient and have difficulty knowing what to do with others' emotions and needs.

Your earlier experiences shaped your ability to:

- be self-reflective: aware of yourself, others, and how you relate

- know and make sense of what you are feeling

- regulate how you react: be aware and flexible in how you react

- allow yourself to be impacted by someone else's perspective

- be attuned to and understand someone else's emotions and experience

- hold your own perspective along with someone else's and respond in a considerate manner

- express understanding, comfort, and care in a meaningful way

- be comfortable with closeness, both emotionally and physically

All the experiences and interactions from your early relationships are internalized and become the lens through which you view yourself, others, and the world around you. Your internalized ways of relating become the pattern or grid for your way of being and responding in relationships. These patterns shape your perspective, beliefs, and expectations regarding how to love and react when you feel disconnected. Your particular internal lens informs what you expect from love, how you love, and what hurts when you love. In this way, you view life from inside your tunnel. This lens colors everything you see and gives the meaning to all your interactions.

As you grow older, all your significant and influential relationships continually shape how you view the world and relate to others. When you marry you bring to the marriage your established patterns of relating that continually mold and shape how you connect with, respond to, and love your spouse.

THE HEALING POWER OF BEING LOVED

Marriage can either confirm your internal lens and old patterns of relating or create opportunities for new and healthier experiences and patterns. It is amazing how God uses marriage as a place where you are not only refined but also healed. When your spouse connects with you emotionally, he or she becomes part of the healing process of your old childhood wounds.

Sadly, many people see their partners the same way they have experienced everyone else in their lives:

- "I knew you wouldn't be there for me; no one was there for me growing up."
- "My parents never paid attention to me unless I performed or fussed, and neither do you."
- "My parents were busy people and not there for me, so I became self-sufficient. It's best to be independent in the marriage as well. It's not only safer but also more logical."

But the healing balm of the love of your spouse can change how you view yourself as well as how you relate to others. Because of the love, care, and nurturing of your spouse, new ways of being in relationship can arise:

- "My father was harsh, always finding what I did wrong, but my husband's understanding helped me realize I am worthwhile."
- "My mother was moody and ignored me; my wife is gentle and predictable, allowing me to come close and trust the care of someone else."

The way you relate to your spouse either confirms their fears about whether or not they are deeply loved or is part of a new experience that heals and replaces their old negative experiences.

WE ARE ALL JUST *FIGHTING* FOR LOVE

As you have discovered in this chapter, when we sense that our spouse is not available or responsive, the relationship system sounds the alarms, triggering strong emotions. We then go through a sequence of reactions: We protest with anger and hope. If that doesn't reunite us with our spouse, we feel sad and despaired. And finally we cope by defensively emotionally detaching.

When we perceive our spouse to not be accessible or responsive, our hurt and longing to be close is often mixed with fear, anger, frustration, and defensiveness. As a result, the tender relationship-related longings, needs, and fears (such as, "I love you," "I miss you," "I was hurt by you") often get lost in our defensive ways of reacting.[7]

For example, the feeling of "I miss you and, even though I am capable of doing life without you, I prefer to do life with you," comes out as, "Where have you been? You are home late from the office—again!" In the middle of a heated argument, husbands and wives react out of their anger of hope, sadness, and detachment, and their tender heart that says, "I long for you, wish you were closer, more under-standing and considerate," often gets lost.

Distressed couples escalate their arguments by reacting in negative ways when their relationship system alarms sound off. Couples stay in these negative emotional states as long as they continue to perceive that the other is not available or responsive, and this creates distress in a marriage. Yet in the midst of our hurt and anger, we argue in *hopes* of being seen, heard, and understood. We just long to be close and connected with our spouse.

In the next chapter I will share the "attachment styles," or ways of being in a relationship that shape and impact our interactions. Then in the following chapter, I will describe the physiology of our relationship alarm system and what is actually happening in our brains and bodies when we sense our spouse is not there for us. When you understand why you react the way you do when you're hurt, you are able to choose different ways of responding—ways that help your spouse hear what you are *really* trying to say.

QUESTIONS AND EXERCISES

1. When growing up, were your parents physically around and available? How emotionally available were your parents? How did they comfort you when you were sad or hurt? How did they come back and reconnect with you when you got into trouble? How do you feel your early experiences have impacted you as an adult today?

2. What kind of safe haven have you and your spouse been for each other over the course of your marriage? That is, have you had quality time together, built trust, been emotionally and physically available to each other, responded to each other in a considerate manner, and repaired your arguments in constructive ways?

3. Sometimes we get angry in hopes of our spouse seeing our hurts and doing something about it. Think back on the last few times you and your spouse argued. How did your anger of hope come into play?

THREE DRAGONS AND VULNERABILITIES

The Hidden Meanings that Fuel Our Arguments

IT WAS MIDWAY THROUGH THE FIRST DAY OF WHAT SEEMED to be a very productive marriage intensive with Ray and April. After lunch I walked into the waiting room to see if they were ready to resume the afternoon session and found the couple sitting on the couch warmly chatting with each other. I was moved by how caring they seemed to be toward each other. "I'll be right with you," I said, as I went to grab a fresh notepad from the storage shelf.

When I returned, I was surprised. In less than three minutes the atmosphere in the waiting room had drastically changed. Ray was leaning forward, emitting a big sigh as he rubbed his frowning forehead. April's face was red as she kept muttering to Ray while frantically attempting to put a lid on her coffee cup.

What happened? In less than three minutes a war had broken out!

Once they settled in my office, I had to ask, "What happened in the waiting room?"

April: "Ask him, he's the one who got all upset."

Ray: "I was just sitting perfectly happy until she got mad."

April: "Mad? All I did was ask him to get us lids for our
coffee cups."

Ray: "I got her the lids, and she was still not happy."

April: "All I said was, 'My coffee is hot; please get me a
coffee lid.' You just sat there glaring at me—like you
always do when I ask you for help."

Ray: "This always happens. She gets angry and I end up
being the bad guy."

Why would coffee-cup lids trigger a response reserved for major
betrayals and injustices? This is about coffee-cup lids, for goodness'
sake, not losing a month's paycheck while gambling at the race-
track! Why such a big reaction?

I am sure you and your spouse also have had small, harmless events
become bigger than life, starting an argument that quickly became
heated. These simple and very typical encounters often escalate into
huge arguments because they are connected to deeper meanings and
fears. Because of these connections, seemingly innocuous everyday
interactions have the potential to trigger our relationship alarm system
and set in motion reactions that are both physiologically and emotionally powerful.

During these arguments, there is a sudden shift from *what* you
are arguing about to *why* you are arguing. The argument is no
longer just about ordinary events, such as asking for coffee-cup lids,
but rather about deeper meanings, fears, vulnerabilities, and sensitivities that are triggered by the coffee-cup lids of our own lives.

WHEN WHAT YOU ARGUE ABOUT IS NOT WHAT YOU ARE ARGUING ABOUT

I'm sure you can write a whole list of things that you and your
spouse argue about. These *topics* are probably the same most couples
would list: money, sex, time together, division of household chores,
children, in-laws, religious matters, and the "right" or "proper" way
of doing things. These arguments play out in daily events, such as

coming home late, not taking out the trash, or disagreements over what TV programs your child can watch. These events often have deeper meanings attached to them, and because of this, what we argue about is not always what we are arguing about.

Each week in the counseling room, I open with "Good to see you. So, how was your week?" In response I hear about the events concerning a particular topic. Each couple has *hot topics* that are most hurtful or irritating to them. If a couple's hot topics are money and division of household chores, then most of the arguments will start with legitimate complaints concerning an event surrounding those particular hot topics, such as who spent what money and who did not help with certain chores. But very quickly the argument will shift to the *meaning* of the event.

Topic: *We don't agree on financial issues.*
Event: *"You forgot to record the amount of the check you wrote."*
Meaning: *"You are not a team player and don't care about the goals we set. I am alone, and everything is up to me."*

What your spouse did or said comes to mean more than what happened. In the middle of an argument you suddenly realize, *This is not just about the checks.* There is a deeper layer of complex factors contributing to and fueling the seemingly mundane argument regarding checks, trash, coffee-cup lids, children, and in-laws.

INFLUENCES THAT SHAPE THE MEANINGS

The meanings surrounding these events were shaped by various influences in your life, including personality and temperament, personal lifestyle preferences, and most importantly, your past hurts.

Personality and Temperament

First, your *personality and temperament* become part of the lens through which you view life and impact what you perceive to be the right way of doing something or what is hurtful. We are each born with a personality, a way of being that makes up the essence of who we are.

Some people are born leaders, outgoing and always focused on getting things done. I call these people *greens*. They tend to get down to business. But because of the way they are, greens become irritated at slower paced, easygoing people and often feel others are holding them back, slowing them down, or being intentionally lazy. The bright and fun-loving *reds*, on the other hand, often feel their joys are stifled by schedules, rules, and structure. The goal-oriented greens, however, believe that structure is absolutely essential. *Blues* focus on planning and can't believe anyone doesn't start their day without writing and reviewing a good list. They are frustrated by those who don't look at the potential downside to all situations. *Yellows* are good listeners, patient, and loyal, but they avoid conflict and don't understand why everyone can't be more easygoing, flexible, and appreciative of the status quo.

Your unique personality gives you a certain rhythm in life and your own way of viewing the world around you. It impacts how you express your emotions, how you approach your work and goals, as well as your needs and hurts in relationships. What does not fit your "mold" often feels out of place, unnatural, even hurtful. For instance, when an easygoing yellow resists change, she is actually responding out of her natural bent rather than squelching and sabotaging plans for something different. A red is not intentionally leaving projects undone but sometimes gets distracted by the moment and the possibilities of new projects. A blue just wants to make sure plans are well thought through and all the negatives taken into consideration; she really doesn't intend to put a damper on the excitement. Nor is a green out to control and win but rather is focused on the goal and getting the job done.

The Color of Your Personality*

Red

__ fun loving __ energetic __ emotionally expressive

__ spontaneous __ a cheerleader __ talks too much

__ can't remember details __ restless energy

__ forgets obligations __ starts but doesn't finish projects

__ prefers to be with others

Green

__ leader __ focused __ likes control __ goal oriented

__ gets the job done __ independent __ type A

__ dislikes emotions __ insensitive to others __ knows everything

__ can't say, "Sorry, I was wrong" __ dominates others

Blue

__ planner __ analytical __ serious, deep thinker __sensitive

__ self-sacrificing __ orderly, likes charts and lists __ problem solver

__ often feels alone, hurt __ hesitant to start projects

__ sees the negative side

Yellow

__ easygoing __ patient __ consistent, goes with flow

__ agreeable __ would rather watch __ worries

__ prefers to support and stay in background

__ avoids responsibility __ indecisive __ indifferent to plans

__ avoids change

* There are many well-researched personality inventories; this is just a fun and simple way of understanding your and your spouse's personalities.

Lifestyle Preferences

The second group of influences that shape what meaning you give a situation are *lifestyle preferences*. Your life preferences and ways of doing things seem the "normal" or "proper" way of life. These might be your natural tastes and likes, or often they come from the influence of your early family and culture. When you were growing up, how things were done, organized, and celebrated became a part of you, and now you feel that these are the proper ways of doing things. For example, Christmas Eve just seems the *right* time to open presents and exchange gifts. Anything else seems out of place and, well, almost wrong.

Past Hurts

The third influence that shapes the meaning events take on are your *painful past relationship experiences*. There were times when you were hurt and vulnerable, and these pains left soft spots or tender places in your life. Perhaps your father left on business trips for extended periods of time and when he was around, you would never know when he'd be up and gone again. You now are sensitive to your husband's absences. Or maybe your stepmother would choose her own children over you and your brother. You are now sensitive to anything that feels like favoritism and what is not fair.

DRAGONS, VULNERABILITIES, AND TENDER PLACES

I have come to call the tender places in our hearts left by past hurts, fears, and vulnerabilities our *dragons*. Experiences we have had over the course of our lives create and shape what our vulnerabilities are today. When experiences in your relationships today are similar to the hurtful experiences you had over the course of your life, they trigger the same hurts, fears, and responses. When a current situation touches or raises your old hurts and sets in motion your automatic way of reacting to those hurts, your "dragons have been raised."

Experiences over your lifetime ▶	Become your "dragons" today
Past hurts, fears	your sensitive spot
What made you feel scared,	your vulnerabilities
alone, vulnerable, unloved,	what you fear
misunderstood, disrespected	what hurts

Simply put, when something happens today that touches the *vulnerable spot* of our old hurts or fears, our *dragons are raised,* and we respond in the same automatic way that we responded when we originally experienced that hurt. We are often not aware of this process because we don't realize that it is our old hurt and our automatic way of responding to defend or protect ourselves from the hurt that is shaping how we view a situation and fueling our response. This unawareness on our part gives our dragons a powerful hold on what we perceive as hurtful and the way we respond and argue with our spouse.

For example, if while growing up you felt that no one was there for you and you had to take care of yourself, you will probably feel the same way when your spouse fails to do something that is important to you. And if you reacted to this sense of "I'm on my own" by becoming anxious and attempting to win the favor of your parent by performing, you will probably also seek the emotional attention of your spouse by trying to please and do more for your spouse.

How you responded then . . . ▶	Shapes how you automatically react today when your dragons are raised.

Your Dragons and Relationship System

As I said earlier, most often we argue with our spouse about everyday events. What happens, though, is that these everyday events often touch our vulnerable places, our soft spot, our fears, and old hurts. And when they do, our dragons rise up, warning us that our haven is not so safe, and our relationship alarm system sounds off. We are then ready to react in a way that protects and defends our heart and attempts to restore the relationship.

Darin's experience will show you how this works. When Darin was growing up, his father would criticize and shame him if he did anything his dad disapproved of. Darin learned to cope with his dad's harsh and rejecting words by lowering his head, shutting down on the inside, and hiding in his bedroom the rest of the night. Now as an adult, whenever Darin hears someone belittling him (or anything that slightly resembles a belittling remark), he feels bad about himself and automatically hides and shrinks away. It is hard for him to speak his mind in those situations. His past experiences—or dragons—have taught him well. Now every time he perceives a put-down, his alarm sounds off, warning him of the situation that could potentially cause shame, and he responds automatically.

He hears a put-down ♦ *his dragons are raised* ♦
relationship system alarms sound off ♦ *he reacts by*
withdrawing and shrinking away

So when the trash not being taken out comes to mean "you are not there for me," then the sight of the trash overflowing is perceived as more than just a mess. It is experienced as a slight, a rejection, a disrespect followed by your relationship system asking your spouse, "Are you emotionally available and responsive? Are you my safe haven?" If the answer is no or "I am uncertain," then the alarms of your relationship system sound off, and the relationship system will attempt to restore the rupture.

Topics	Daily Events	What It Means/What Dragon It Raises
Money	Spouse did not record amount of the checks.	I do everything; you're not there for me.
Children	Spouse lets kids watch inappropriate movie.	You are insensitive to what I value; I care for the kids alone.
In-laws	Spouse invited them without asking me.	I am on my own; I'm not a priority to you.
Chores	Spouse didn't help with dishes voluntarily.	I do everything; I'm not considered.

Where do our hurts, vulnerabilities, and tender places that trigger our dragons first get formed? To gain a broader understanding of our dragons, let's go back to the beginning and look at how our earlier relationship experiences created our dragons and shaped the lens through which we view life.

As I discussed in chapter 2, our attachment system impacts how we love and react in our marriage relationship today. Our early experiences with our parents are internalized and influence how we relate in our current marriage relationship. This *way of being* in a relationship is called an *attachment style*, or what I refer to in this book as our "relationship style." Our relationship style gives us insight to what are our vulnerabilities, fears, hurts, and sensitive places in our hearts—or our dragons.

Attachment Relationship Styles

There are four basic relationships styles that have been identified in the study and research on attachment: *secure, anxious-preoccupied, avoidant,* and *fearful avoidant.* These are not hard and fast categories, but guides that shed light on what our vulnerabilities might be, helping us become more aware of the lens through which we view the world around us.

ATTACHMENT STYLES

Secure	Anxious-Preoccupied
Comfortable getting close	Anxious about availability of others
Feel lovable and that others are reliable	Work hard to be seen and noticed
See others as trustworthy and caring	Worry about relationships
Confident that conflicts can be resolved	Long to be connected; afraid others won't want to be close as well
Trust the intentions of others	

Avoidant	Fearful Avoidant
Independent and self-sufficient	Long for love but afraid others will hurt and let them down
Substitute things and goals for love and connection	Often perceive themselves as unworthy
Uncomfortable with emotions	Fear spouse will leave if they really knew them
Experienced lots of rejection	

Secure Attachment Relationship Style

Early attachment relationship patterns. Parents with a secure attachment way of being in relationships are emotionally available, nurturing, attuned, and responsive to their children. They are able to understand their child's needs and can meet them in a "good enough" manner. These parents are generally able to perceive their child's signals of distress, make sense of what the signals mean, and respond appropriately in a timely and effective manner, developing for their child a safe haven to turn to and find comfort. This inner sense of security becomes the secure base from which a child confidently ventures out into the world.

It didn't have to be perfect all the time, but if your parents were mostly attuned and responsive to your needs, your chances were increased that you felt lovable and that others would be able and willing to give you the love you longed for. This in turn laid a foundation for an inner sense of security, self-worth, and confidence—increasing your chances of getting along with friends, having fewer behavioral problems, and being more resilient in emotional situations.

Adult secure pattern of being in relationships. Securely attached husbands and wives are comfortable being close to their spouse. They often say, "I don't worry about being alone or not getting the love I need from my spouse." As a result, the lens through which securely attached husbands and wives look at life and relationships finds others lovable and relationships manageable.

It's not that they haven't suffered hurts, developed tender spots and vulnerabilities, or developed their own sensitivities. They have. Certainly these couples get upset, mad, disappointed, and even argue vehemently. But the difference is that they are confident their spouse will listen to their complaints and respond, and in turn, they do the same. They don't need to react in an escalating, contemptuous, and destructive way in order to be heard and understood.

Secure couples are able to listen and respond to the emotional needs of their spouse. Difficulties and differences are faced with the hope that they will be resolved, and therefore, hurts don't accumulate. No matter what happens, secure couples will attempt to consider each other's perspective and respond in the best interest of the relationship.

Anxious-Preoccupied Relationship Attachment Style

Early attachment relationship patterns. Parents who are anxiously attached have good intentions to be there for their children but are often inconsistent. At times these parents are emotionally available and present and at other times are unresponsive, possibly overprotective, or even emotionally intrusive. Sometimes they're attuned and sensitive to their child's needs; other times they're tired, irritated, or frustrated and respond in an impatient or less-caring manner.

Anxious parents can also be overwhelmed and not sure how to handle the challenges of parenting and become overprotective, fostering fear, worry, anxiety, and clinginess in a child.

Children with anxious parents learn that they can't depend upon their loved ones for consistent connection. This leaves them with a sense of anxiety and uncertainty about whether or not they can get the care and comfort needed from their parent. This uncertainty creates a general feeling of insecurity and anxiety in relationships, making it difficult for them to feel consistently safe or loved by their parent.

Adult anxious pattern of being in relationships. People with anxious patterns want to be close, but worry whether their spouse wants to be as close as they do, saying, "Sometimes I feel close and loved by my spouse; other times I don't. And I work hard to keep our connection."

To be noticed and obtain the attention of their loved one, anxious people learn to react in one of three ways. One way is to become dependent, clingy, and fearful of venturing out. They also fear rejection, criticism, or embarrassment.

Another way is to be constantly onstage in an attempt to be seen, noticed, and reassured of being worthy and wanted. In hopes of being noticed, their reactions become big and emotional when they feel hurt or when the connection between them and their loved one is threatened.

The third way anxious people attempt to get the love they long for is by pleasing others. They aim to do what they can to keep the peace and make their spouse happy, such as offering an apology whenever they feel their spouse is getting upset. You will find anxious husbands or wives saying, "I just want to be close to you." They also become anxious when they can't reach their spouse or when they're disconnected due to arguments or a busy schedule.

Avoidant Relationship Attachment Styles

Early attachment relationship patterns. Wyatt's parents loved him dearly, although they tended to be harsh, cold, physically unaffectionate, unsympathetic, and emotionally disconnected with him. Parents like this are not able to manage or even allow their child's expression of emotions, therefore they offer limited comfort. Consequently, Wyatt learned to stuff his own feelings and needs and became self-sufficient and independent. In doing so, he developed an avoidant way of being in relationships.

Elissa recalls standing in the bathroom as a child, bleeding from her knee and hearing her mother say, "Stand up straight before I really give you something to cry about. This is nothing. I will take you to the hospital someday and there you will see people who are really hurt." Elissa admits that she never learned to deal with her own feelings, never mind knowing how to comfort others.

Adult avoidant pattern of being in relationships. The way of being in adult relationships for avoidants like Wyatt and Elissa is to be independent and self-sufficient. Their lens of viewing relationships is that, although others are capable of being loving, they will reject you when you need them the most. The avoidant concludes, "Relationships are fine, but I am comfortable not being very close to others. It is important to be self-sufficient and independent. I am not emotionally dependent on my spouse and don't expect my spouse to be dependent on me."

An avoidant spouse feels worthy of love and capable of getting the love he or she needs but feels that others won't be there. An avoidant comes to a resolve of, "I don't need much, so it's okay." Avoidants figure things out on their own and don't turn toward their spouse for emotional support. Work, addictions, hobbies, or other distractions often become a source of self-soothing and a substitute for love and connectedness.

Avoidants conclude, as Wyatt did, that "emotions only get in the way, and it is best to be logical and face the nuts and bolts of life rather than fuss about all the mush and feelings. Anyway, it's weak to be needy or sad." Since an avoidant has not had his needs, longings, and emotions seen, made sense of, and responded to, he does not know what to do with them when they arise in himself or others. Therefore, he becomes uncomfortable, overwhelmed, or perplexed in vulnerable, tender, or emotional moments. As soon as his spouse expresses a hurt or need, an avoidant tends to pull back and either switch into problem-solving mode, neutralize his emotions, or shut down. An avoidant often says, "Well, what do you want me to do about it?" or, "Don't cry; it does nothing for me except make me angry." Or when a wife asks her avoidant husband to be more emotionally available, he answers, "What are you talking about? I don't know what you want from me!"

Fearful Avoidant Relationship Attachment Style

Early relationship attachment patterns. Children learn to be fearful and avoidant when growing up in abusive, neglectful, or emotionally unpredictable homes. Their parents' emotional availability and responsiveness is based on their own mood or needs, causing them to be not only inconsistent and unpredictable in the love they give, but often abusive. These children often experience their parents as frightening or hurtful instead of caring and comforting.

Hannah recalls coming home each day after school, fearing what "face" her mom would have on that day. If Mom was sober, she was caring and interested in Hannah. But if Mom was in a depressive or drunken episode, then her fuse was short, and anything and everything would irritate her and warrant a spanking with the belt. Hannah recalls living in fear of her mother yet looking forward to the days when she was given permission to curl up on Mom's lap and sing songs. Hannah was just unsure when those moments would be.

Adult fearful avoidant ways of being in relationships. Spouses who are fearful avoidants long to be close and connected but fear being hurt if they are. When their relationship alarm system sounds off saying, "You are hurt and scared; run to the comfort of your safe haven," they are stuck in a dilemma. Previous relationship experience tells them that their safe haven is both the source of pain as well as the source of comfort.

The harsh and emotionally inconsistent experiences that fearful avoidants have had with their caregivers are internalized, and the lens through which they view their relationships says, "I want to be emotionally close, but I have difficulty trusting or depending on my spouse completely. I worry that I will eventually be hurt or let down if I become too close."

Perceiving themselves as unworthy and unlovable, these husbands and wives often say, "Some days I can't believe my wife loves me and is still with me." They believe that their spouse would leave if they really knew them. They try hard to get close and please their spouse, yet they are unable to get their spouse's love and attention and end up feeling their efforts have fallen short. Fearful avoidants have a push-pull, come-close-no-not-that-close way of being. They constantly scan the horizon to see whether or not their spouse is there for them and wait for the spouse to disappoint and let them down. Arguments are around "Everything you do proves that you don't love me or care for me. I'm not a priority; I never have been, and I never will be." Arguments often leave fearful avoidants feeling hopeless about their relationship and spouse.

COFFEE-CUP LIDS: THE REST OF THE STORY

Remember Ray and April in the opening story? Their coffee-cup-lids encounter sounded their relationship alarms, triggered their dragons, and started an argument . . . within seconds. Let's understand their attachment styles and what dragons were fueling their ordinary encounter, turning it into a heated argument. Here's the rest of the story behind their argument.

April asked Ray to get her a coffee-cup lid, and it triggered in him a powerful reaction. To understand a bit more about Ray's dragons, we begin by looking at the significant experiences he had growing up.

Ray grew up in a chaotic home. Ray's stepmother was harsh, always demanding Ray to do something for her. If Ray objected, he would get a spanking from his stepmother and another when his father got home from work for "upsetting his stepmother." Ray explains, "I was never asked, 'Please help me peel the potatoes.' It was a command laced with a threat, 'You'd better peel the potatoes or else.' As a result, Ray's relationship style is more avoidant. He feels his advances for love will be rejected. His dragons say, "Those closest to you only want you close because of what you can do for them."

Today when Ray hears April panic and say, "Quick, Ray, get me a lid—this coffee is spilling," her request sounds more like a demand, triggering his dragons. Feeling angry and resentful inside, Ray gives April a cold stare as he slowly complies with what she has asked.

However, Ray's cold stare and his seeming unwillingness to help raise April's dragons and trigger her relationship alarms. Her dragons tell her that she is a burden and bother to Ray and that her needs are not important to him, just as she felt with her father growing up. April's relationship style is more anxious, and she feels she can only get the attention of others if she panics and makes her reactions big and dramatic. Ray doesn't feel like a safe haven to her—and she lets him know.

HOW DRAGONS ARE STORED IN OUR MEMORIES

To discover what past events have created our dragons, we can take a trip down memory lane and review our growing up years and interactions with our parents. Even though you don't remember all your past childhood experiences, they still have an impact on your present. As I explain how, I must warn you: I'm going to use a few vocabulary words reminiscent of your biology class in school, but hang in there with me. I am certain it will add to your understanding of how you and your spouse argue.

An important part of the brain relevant to arguing is the *hippocampus*, which is the memory center. Your hippocampus stores information coming in from your senses along with the emotional experience that comes in from another part of your brain, called the *amygdala*. The *amygdala* (pronounced a-MIG-dah-lah) is the part of your brain that adds emotional meaning to all your experiences. The memory center (*hippocampus*) stores factual and contextual information, while the emotional brain (*amygdala*) stores the feelings linked with a particular situation. When you were hurt or scared as a child, you reacted and responded in a particular way. How you felt when these experiences happened, as well as the way you responded, were stored together in your brain.

So if your mother repeatedly failed to pick you up from school on time, your memory center stored the facts regarding the times you were left standing alone on the sidewalk after school long after all the other kids had been picked up by their parents. But it was your emotional brain that washed your experience with emotional meaning: scared, abandoned, and angry.

What is amazing is that you don't have to remember your childhood event to feel the rush of emotion in the middle of an argument. That's because our memories are stored in two different ways.

1. *Explicit memory* stores facts and visual images of an event, along with the emotional feelings associated with that event.

2. *Implicit memory* remembers sensations. There is no recall of details regarding the event, just how you felt. Your

memory banks may or may not store all the factual
details of the past event (the image of you standing on
the sidewalk alone), but your emotional brain will
remember that when such events happened, you felt sad,
fearful, and abandoned. In the future, any situation that
slightly resembles being left alone will trigger the same
sad and fearful emotional reaction.

When Hurts Today Feel Familiar

Staying with the example of being picked up late from school,
the experience of standing on the sidewalk alone was stored with
the emotional experience of being scared, angry, abandoned, and
alone. What if you were unable to share your fear and hurt with
your mother? Instead, when she finally picked you up, you held
back the tears as you sat quietly in the backseat of the car. Now
anything that resembles this past hurt or painful experience triggers a similar emotion and response in you today. So when your
spouse is late, you may or may not have the "picture memory" of
standing on the sidewalk waiting for your mother, but your emotional brain will remember the emotions associated with being left
alone, and you feel the same surge of fear and anger you felt when
your mom was late. You feel hurt and angry, but you say nothing
and sulk all day.

Reacting Out of Our Dragons

Our dragons are often raised so quickly that we often don't con-
sciously make the connection between the past event and our current
vulnerability. But something in us automatically reacts a particular
way because it feels like the safest and most familiar way of protecting ourselves.

For example, when you feel manipulated, you sulk to change your spouse's behavior. Sulking is familiar because your father would do it often. Or when you feel demeaned, you lash back with sarcasm as you did at school whenever you got teased; your brothers did it at home, so you learned to do it well. Or if you feel ignored, you pursue and get louder just as you did when you tried to get your father's attention while growing up. The hurts that raise their heads trigger automatic responses within us.

On the other hand, some people respond contrary to the way they did as a child. For example, instead of keeping the hurt and anger inside, you now explode. The anger and hurt you could not express to your parent now comes out in an unmanaged and often hurtful manner.

The catch is that the way you reacted to your pain when you were young may not work in your relationship today. Responding in your old automatic way is often hurtful, pushing your spouse away rather than increasing understanding and connectedness. Your ability to shut out the world and go into the backyard and daydream to stay out of trouble served you well while growing up. But doing the same when your wife criticizes you does not solve the concerns in your marriage. Or if you got angry and yelled to be heard in your alcoholic family, doing it now only wounds your spouse and your safe haven—*and it doesn't get you heard.*

So if all these reactions are "programmed" into our brains, how do we learn to react differently and in ways that will help us to be heard and understood? Well, it is a journey to discover that the way you react is not necessary to get your spouse to come close and listen, and you've already begun by reading this book. In chapter 8 I will show you some practical steps to help you continue the journey. Meanwhile, you'll find the next chart helpful as you think about your own childhood situations and how you learned to react.

How did you view yourself and others?
What hurt you, and how did you react?

Here are some descriptive words to help you out.

Viewed Myself	Viewed Others	What Hurt Me	How I Reacted
Lovable	Able to love me	Left alone a lot	Left the situation
Unworthy	Willing to love me	Neglected	Argued
The hero	Unavailable	Abused	Became self-sufficient
The black sheep	Emotional	Rejected	Avoided strong emotion
Special	Unpredictable	Not seen	Did things to please
Crybaby	Caring, always there	Not respected	Became silent
Rejected	Rejecting	Belittled	Fearful, worried
Alone	Punishing	Ignored	Got angry
Self-sufficient	Loyal	No comfort	Cried a lot

When You and Your Spouse Create Your Own Dragons

Of course, our dragons aren't created *only* by our childhood experiences. Over the years of marriage, new dragons are created by hurts inflicted by our spouse. There are times when he or she is not there for us, lets us down, or is insensitive. Often these everyday inconsequential moments are folded into our experience and accepted as human foibles. We might say, "Hey, that hurt when you said that," and our spouse hears and responds in a caring manner.

But there are times when our spouse wounds us in a deep way, creating a hurt that is remembered and shapes future interactions. These hurts become the dragons you have created together.

For example, if your wife promises to pay the bills on time, but consistently fails to do so, your trust in her dependability begins to falter. And each time she says, "I will take care of that, I promise," you cringe, thinking, *Yeah, right; I usually end up doing it myself. I don't think you will follow through on your word, so I'd better not trust you.*

Other Hurtful Life Experiences That Create Dragons

In addition to our childhood and marital hurts, there are other life experiences that shape the meaning we give to events. What you experience in play, work, and the world around you impacts how safe you feel and the meaning you give to situations today. Losses, especially if they were complicated, impact how you view the world. Rosalyn lost her mother a few days before her wedding. The day after her first baby was born, her husband lost his job. She now feels as though all the joys in life come on the heels of deep pain and anticipates something bad happening around the good events of life.

Some give their whole hearts to their spouse, only to have their marriage end in an ugly divorce. Now, although they long to be loved, they are cautious about risking and are afraid of trusting another person. The fear of being hurt keeps them alert and protected.

If you have had a painful or rejecting experience at work, your hurts impact the lens through which you view the emotional safety of others. A senior pastor of a large church once told me, "When the church split and people I thought were my closest confidants and friends left, I was shattered. Trusting people again has been difficult. I fear that no matter how close people promise to be, when their agenda doesn't match what I can offer, they leave."

BAD MANNERS

After one of my conferences, a wife came up to me and said, "Dr. Morris May, I have been digging to discover what my husband's dragons are, but all I can find are bad manners."

Sometimes, like all couples, we are easily irritated and react with plain old bad manners. We become inconsiderate, rude, disrespectful, ill-mannered, impolite, or offensive. We forget to be considerate and treat each other as our greatest treasure. Some of the ways you forget to use manners might be: You don't get off the phone to say hello when your husband comes home from work. You don't call your wife to find out how her doctor's appointment went. You grunt when your wife asks you a question. When your husband gets in your way, you rudely say, "Get out; I can't get dinner ready with you bugging me." When your wife walks in front of the TV when the football scores are shown, you yell, "Not now! Do you mind? Step aside. Can't I get a moment of peace?!" You no longer thank your wife for the dinner she made or show appreciation for your husband when he balances the checkbook. After years of marriage, politeness often fades. Many couples feel their spouse will always be there no matter how they react to them in the small things. And many husbands and wives feel justified in the way they react. But at the end of each day, very few couples review how polite or well-mannered they were with each other.

Review your attitudes and actions. Are they fueled by dragons, hurts, and vulnerabilities? Or are they the result of plain old bad manners?

BLINDED BY MY OWN DRAGONS

One night Carlos was walking down the hallway, eager to go out to dinner with his wife, when he heard her yell out from the bathroom, "Did you switch the light off in the garage?" Instead of answering, "Thanks for the reminder; I already did," something inside him snapped. He suddenly felt as belittled as he did when his mother hovered over him as a child, always doubting his ability to do anything right. He walked past the bathroom shaking his head, thinking, *Who does she think I am? A child? Stupid? Of course I turned the light off!* And out of his mouth came a sarcastic and blaming remark: "What do you think? I don't leave the lights on like you do!" In the moment he felt justified reacting that way. *After all,* he thought, *if my wife didn't say what she says, I would not react the way I do.* But as he lay in bed that night he wondered, *Why did I react so harshly to my wife's simple question?*

Like Carlos, many couples are unaware of why they react the way they do. They perceive they are reacting only to the situation in front of them, unaware of the unseen dragons and vulnerabilities that fuel their reactions.

What are your dragons and vulnerabilities that come to mean "You are not there for me"? What are some things that have the strength to trigger powerful reactions in you, setting in motion strong patterns of arguing?

Our dragons limit our choices for reacting because they put into motion automatic responses that may or may not be relationship enhancing. For example, if your mother was controlling, maybe you have come into adulthood having a negative reaction to anything that feels controlling. Your dragons say, "No one will control me," and if you feel someone is acting in a controlling way, you fight for yourself by shutting out your spouse.

Growing is when you begin to recognize your dragons and the ways you react when your dragons are triggered. You are able to step back, not be driven by those dragons, but understand why a particular situation has such power over your emotions and reactions.

Your and My Dragons Are Our Problems

Living with each other's dragons can be difficult. Many couples don't know what their spouses' dragons are or what to do when those dragons arise. They only know that their spouses react in hurtful ways. And for lack of anything else to blame, they blame the way their spouse was raised.

Esther complains that Samuel is overly sensitive because of his critical father, and Samuel complains that Esther is controlling because of her alcoholic mother. Samuel laments, "How long must I go on paying the price for what her mother did to her? That happened a long time ago; this is now. Just get over it." Esther says, "Why should I have to put up with the way he protects himself because of how his father treated him? I get punished for what his father did to him."

In marriage we walk alongside our spouses as they wrestle to understand the power of their dragons and find healing and growth. We walk together as we learn new and more Christlike ways of relating. On the journey to maturity, we become part of each other's growth and healing, offering comfort and encouragement as we each try to understand our dragons and learn not to allow them to control our lives. We need to remember that we are part of each other's journey as God completes the good work He has begun in each of us.

Giving Each Other New Experiences of Being Loved

There are incredible opportunities for you and your spouse to impact each other on a very deep level and become a part of healing your past hurts. When your spouse responds in a caring and considerate manner instead of the negative way you were used to growing up, this new experience changes the lens through which you view life, yourself, and others.

Bonnie shared with me a great example of this. She said, "My father would get very angry and irritated if I ever forgot something or took him out of his way. He would yell and then withdraw his attention as a way of punishing me. I was always scared of getting into trouble. I remember when my husband and I went on our first vacation. We were five miles down the road, and he said to me, 'Hand me the maps.' I searched around to discover that I had left them on the kitchen counter. I was so nervous and scared to tell him, 'I left the maps at home.' But he said calmly, 'Oh, no. Well, okay, we'll get off at the next exit and turn around.' He was disappointed but not angry. I was shocked. I asked why he was not angry. He calmly answered, 'Well, it can happen to anyone. We were rushing to get ready. I could have forgotten just as well as you.' He reacted totally opposite of my father. His patience and caring responses made me less afraid of being wrong."

As husband and wife, you have the awesome opportunity to be each other's safe haven—to love each other by being emotionally and physically available and responding to each other with care, consideration, and good manners. You have the opportunity to give each other a new experience of love that heals the past hurts and shapes a new lens, one that views life with loving and caring eyes. In marriage, you also have the incredible opportunity to be part of each other's healing, wholeness, growth, and maturity. The wounds that hurt our hearts can tenderly be healed by the way we love each other.

But sometimes part of that experience includes arguing, so let's continue looking at what really goes on when we argue. What happens to our hearts, minds, and bodies when our relationship alarms go off? We'll discuss that in the next chapter.

QUESTIONS AND EXERCISES

1. List the hot topics in your marriage. What do you argue about most?

2. What kinds of things does your spouse say or do that to you infer to mean, "You are not my safe haven; you are not emotionally available, thoughtful, or responsive"?

3. What are your dragons, vulnerabilities, and tender places?

4. How do you react when your dragons are raised? (For example, do you get angry, yell, pursue, defend, or withdraw?)

5. Go back and answer the above questions from your spouse's perspective.

FOUR ANATOMY OF AN ARGUMENT

What Happens to Our Hearts, Minds, and Bodies
When Our Relationship Alarms Sound Off

JESSICA WATCHED HER HUSBAND, RANDY, TAKE A LARGE box of chocolates out of his briefcase and put it on the sideboard behind the dining room table. *What a wonderful man!* Jessica said to herself with delight. *He knows how I love gifts of chocolate, especially during a rough week like I've just had.* She had warm feelings about Randy.

After dinner, with joy of being the bearer of gifts, Randy said, "I have a surprise. I stopped and got you a box of chocolates on the way home."

Responding with hugs and kisses of appreciation, Jessica ripped off the wrapping and lifted the lid from the box. As her eyes scanned the chocolates, her smile turned to a frown. "If this is for me, where are the caramels?" she asked with disappointment and disgust. "I should have known. You handpicked all the chocolates *you* like and not one of my favorites. You didn't get this for me!" she yelled. "You got it for yourself. I don't believe I fell for it. You don't really care about me. You are so selfish."

"What are you talking about?" a very surprised and hurt Randy asked. That was not the response he anticipated from Jessica. "Selfish? I bring home a box of chocolates, and I am selfish?" Randy's heart began to beat fast, and he could feel his palms begin to sweat, as though defending not only his ability to choose chocolates but also his character.

"Then where are the chocolates I like? All I ask is for you to think of me once in a while," Jessica answered as she threw the box across the table.

Before Randy could formulate a sentence using an "I" statement, he said with pain in his voice, "You are the selfish one; you always focus on the negative. You are impossible to please."

"I am rather easy to please. It just takes you thinking of me for one minute. I am always considering you; you never consider me," Jessica said, forcing back the tears.

And with that Jessica stormed into the kitchen as Randy followed close behind saying, "All I do every day of my life is think of this family, and for doing that I am selfish?"

THE HEAT OF AN ARGUMENT

It's amazing how one moment a box of chocolates can mean, "You are wonderful and thoughtful, and you love me," and the next moment it signifies danger in the relationship: "You are selfish and never consider me."

What happened? Yes, Jessica's dragons were raised at the absence of caramels. But what created in Jessica the strong and powerful reaction that followed?

And why did the one little word *selfish* raise not only Randy's dragons but also his heart rate, triggering a hurtful and defensive reaction?

I'm certain you've had experiences similar to Randy and Jessica's and have probably thought to yourself, *Why do I feel so angered by what my spouse just said?* Or, *Why did my spouse react so strongly to a seemingly small provocation?*

Why do we get caught up in our emotions, no matter how logical we think we are? Why do tender, more empathetic, and emotionally connecting ways of responding seem so foreign when we are caught in the moments of being hurt, angry, or upset?

In this chapter you will find answers to these questions as we look at the neurobiology of an argument. Even though it may seem like a biology lesson at first, it really will help you understand why certain events trigger strong emotional reactions, causing you and your spouse to shift from feeling love and care to hurt and angry . . . in a matter of seconds. Knowing how to do things differently in the heat of an argument first requires an understanding of how our incredible brains work when we are stuck in the spin cycle of our arguments.

EMOTIONS AND YOUR BRAIN

In the heat of the moment, emotions, not logic, have more power over your mind, body, thoughts, and reactions. This might be a surprise to you, but according to research and neuroscientists, it's true.

Dr. Joseph Le Doux, from the Center for Neural Science at New York University, has discovered that information coming in from our senses travels down two different pathways in our brain. One path is the traditional, slower, yet surer, "high road" that leads to our "thinking brain." The other path is the ever quick-and-easy "low road," leading to our "emotional brain." In fact, your emotional brain responds to a situation far more quickly than your thinking brain.

Understanding the high road and low road is important if we want to know why we react so strongly, why we feel so justified reacting the way we do, and why it is so difficult to react differently in the heat of our arguments.

Traveling on the High Road

Information about the world around us comes in through our senses (sight, sound, touch, and other sensory organs) and then these impulses are carried to the *thalamus*. The thalamus is the central station that gathers incoming information and relays it to the different parts of the brain. Typically, all information goes to your brain through the *prefrontal cortex*, or simply the cortex. The cortex area is located right behind your forehead and is considered the "CEO of the brain," the thinking brain, or the area of "second thought." Here, incoming information is looked over and appraised. As part of the prefrontal cortex's due diligence, other parts of the brain are consulted and past experiences stored in the long-term memory banks are reviewed before drawing conclusions and signaling a reaction.

The information is also sent across to the limbic system or the emotional brain, which finds the emotional meaning of the situation and looks for any signs of danger. After such evaluation, the cortex (or thinking brain) determines what an appropriate response should be.

So if you are walking down the street and see someone you recognize, you scan your memories, asking yourself, *Where did I know this person?* Your memory locates the face—it is an old high-school friend. Then the emotion that was stored with your classmate is retrieved. You recall that your old schoolmate was the one who stole your rival school's mascot before the big football game. You chuckle as you recall the hoopla it caused in the local community.

This efficient and orderly high-road path, Dr. Le Doux discovered, is not always the road our experiences travel. In certain situations, the brain takes a neural shortcut and enters what he calls the low road.

Traveling on the Low Road

Dr. Le Doux has discovered that in certain situations that are emotionally laden or perceived to be dangerous either physically or emotionally, the information goes directly from the thalamus to the amygdala, bypassing the cortex. Remember our friend the amygdala from chapter 2, when we were discussing memories that set off alarms? It's a small almond-shaped structure located in our limbic system, otherwise known as the emotional system. I refer to it in this book as the "emotional brain." As you may remember, this emotional alarm center of the brain processes emotional information and adds meaning to all our experiences. When stimulated in the laboratory, the amygdala amazingly produces the emotional reactions of fear, anger, and anxiety.

Assessing for danger. One of the primary jobs of the amygdala is to scan the situation and assess for danger. Your emotional brain rummages through your long-term memory banks trying to find anything that resembles the current situation, asking, *Have I seen this situation in any shape or form before? Is this person, object, or situation bad or dangerous?* If the stimulus is found to be dangerous or slightly resembles a similar past experience you have had, your amygdala sounds off the danger-ahead alarms and signals your body to react by triggering the flow of stress hormones, adrenaline, and noradrenaline. As a result, your heart begins to beat faster to send blood to your muscles, your blood pressure increases, you begin to sweat, and your pupils dilate. In certain cases, you have a startle response, your capacity to feel physical pain is diminished, and your digestive system slows down. Your focus becomes narrow, and all your mind can think about is the danger at hand. Your body gets ready to react to the danger in one of three ways: *fight* what is perceived as dangerous, *flee* from the danger, or *freeze* until the danger passes.

Are you a lover or lion? This stress response serves us well in the face of imminent harm. But what if the danger you perceive is not a jungle lion but your spouse's seemingly inconsiderate remark? What if the fear isn't of your brakes failing on a hill, but your spouse's failure to be home on time as promised? There is no distinction in the emotional brain. And because our relationships mean everything to us, our emotional brain is triggered just as readily when we see a snake as when we sense that our spouse is not there for us. And so the strong physiological reaction we have when we face a lion is similar to when you hear a critical remark and realize your spouse did not consider you. In the face of danger, whether physical or emotional, a person's whole physiological system heads for the emotional low road as it gets ready to attack, run away, or shut down.

THE RELATIONSHIP ALARM SYSTEM

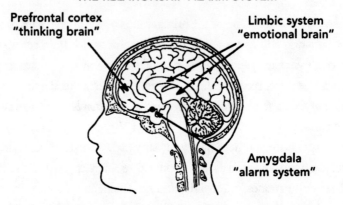

The hijacking. It is important to note that information traveling to the emotional brain travels twice as fast as information traveling on the high road to the thinking brain. Therefore, your emotional brain receives incoming information sooner than your thinking brain. That's why your emotional brain is able to respond more quickly to situations and also has the potential to hijack your higher levels of thinking and reasoning. When this occurs it takes you by surprise, and you find yourself wondering, *What just happened? How did I get here?*

You don't know what hit you.

An angry partner, Gottman's research found, can increase his or her heart rate from ten to thirty beats per second in the space of a single heartbeat. When this happens, you know an amygdala hijacking has occurred.

Behaviors that were correlated with increased physiology or an amygdala hijacking are the same behaviors that Gottman found to predict divorce with 84 percent accuracy: criticism, contempt, defensiveness, and stonewalling. And when couples failed to repair their arguments, Gottman found that the prediction of divorce jumped to 90 percent accuracy.

THE FAST AND FURIOUS LOW ROAD AT WORK

The emotional brain works very fast: within fifteen milliseconds after what you perceive is dangerous, your amygdala processes the information, rapidly scans the situation, and performs a quick pattern recognition. So when your wife says, "You are not going to leave your tools in the middle of the garage, are you?" what she says and how she says it raises your dragon. Her tone of voice sounds critical and her comment belittling.

Your amygdala scans your memories for other situations similar to this one. Then in a split second, without your being aware that it's happening, your brain recalls all the times you were cleaning up your toys when your mother would poke her head in the door and say, "Clean up your mess now," and feeling belittled, you would say to yourself, *I already am; did she really need to say that?* Then you recall the early years of marriage when your wife would constantly follow behind you, telling you the "proper" way to do the dishes or make the beds. Even if what your spouse says *slightly* resembles a past hurtful experience, your amygdala will fire the alarms, priming you to react as if it were certain it had a perfect match. So you react in the automatic and familiar way you know how and sarcastically say to your wife, "I already am; do you really need to be so controlling?"

Upon hearing your comment, your wife is taken by surprise. Unaware that your dragons have raised their heads and sent you directly to the low road, now primed to fight, she concludes you are just plain rude and tells you, "Your sarcasm is unnecessary and uncalled for." Feeling as though she is still hovering, out rolls from your lips the sarcastic words, "Are you going to control every minute of my day off?" But this comment hits her right in her heart. Dead center, it raises her dragons. She is sensitive to being called *controlling* because her mother was, and the last thing she wants to be is like her domineering mother. So her emotional brain sounds off the alarms, and she is ready to fight and defend herself. "I have no interest in telling you what to do or even being with you today." And as she storms into the house and slams the door behind her, you think, *What did I do to get that kind of angry comment?* Oh, the power of an amygdala hijacking!

Tunnel Vision: "I can't hear you"

When our stress response is triggered in the face of perceived danger, we then enter into a state of physiological arousal. This physiological state impacts what we perceive we are seeing or hearing, how we interpret what we are experiencing, and how we're able to process information.

Getting stuck on the low road of the emotional brain can cause tunnel vision. Focus is directed to the danger at hand, and all other interests, information, and feelings are far from interesting. What makes it worse is that once in the tunnel, you interpret everything as a threat. That's because you can only see the situation from your limited perspective and through the lens of your dragon. And your dragon says, "You are not there for me."

When your dragon is raised and your amygdala sounds the danger alarms, you react by protecting yourself and fighting against the perceived danger. You couldn't listen to your spouse if you had to, with your heart racing, your adrenaline pumping, and your emotional brain certain that it perceives danger. Your poor amygdala is doing all it can to help you fight or flee from it!

It's difficult to listen and understand your spouse's perspective and have empathy for his or her feelings when you are in the grips of an amygdala hijacking. Negative emotion is up, and your entire system gets stuck in this powerful physiological state. Your mind can only focus on the danger at hand.

When Your Safe Haven Doesn't Feel So Safe

Triggering Event ▶ *Relationship*
System appraises ▶ *Are you my safe haven?*
encounter, asking: *Are you listening?*
Are you there for me?
Are you available and
responsive?
Do you understand me?

▼

If the answer is:
"I'm not sure" or "No"

▼

Relationship System
sounds the alarms

▼

Dragons are raised

◣

Emotional brain is triggered:
Heart rate goes up
Blood pressure rises
Stress hormones are released
Stress/fear response: *Muscles tense*
fight (attack or defend) *Become focused on "danger."*
flee (withdraw or shut down)
freeze (go numb or do nothing)

Think about it. If the fire alarms suddenly went off in your house, you would not continue to say to your spouse, "Oh, sweetheart, tell me more about how you felt when your boss was critical to you at work." More likely is that the sound of the alarm is going to catch your attention, and your emotional brain is going to get you ready to respond to a perceived danger. You will be more interested in finding out where the fire is than asking how your husband feels about his boss. And you probably are not going to be interested in the rest of his story (never mind being attentive and understanding) until the perceived danger is gone, the alarms have been shut off, and things have settled down.

If your spouse is stuck in an amygdala hijacking, she can't fully hear you, she will not be able to understand you, she won't be able to know what you need or want, and she definitely won't be able to comfort or be there for you. This is why so much damage occurs when a couple is stuck in this fight-or-flight state.

HOW MEN AND WOMEN DIFFER IN THEIR RESPONSES

Men and women generally have different physiological responses to stress and danger, especially when charged up in an argument. Gottman's research found that a husband's physiological response during and after an argument is detrimental to a marriage. When a woman repeatedly pursues and criticizes her husband and his heart rate escalates, research predicts divorce. This doesn't apply the other way around to women. But why would that be?

Men have higher levels of the hormone testosterone, so when physiologically charged in response to stress and danger, they tend to function in a state of vigilance. As a result, it takes them a lot of time to calm down after being so physiologically primed. This makes sense in that over history, men have been wired to stay physiologically vigilant in order to be gatekeepers, to hunt and protect.

Women, on the other hand, were designed with higher levels of the hormone oxytocin, which equips them to want to socialize, be caregivers and nurturers, especially when under stress. Women have a higher ability to help themselves calm down. The testosterone in men, combined with their different stress-coping skills, requires men to take a bit more time to get the stress hormones to calm down their bodies.

Women were also found to be sadder when presented with a complaint in the marriage relationship, and men report being angrier when presented with the same complaint. The conclusion is that women tend to pursue connecting and nurturing and are more sensitive to sadness and loss. On the other hand, men tend to be more attuned to defending and protecting and, under stress, get angry and attack. Obviously these gender differences cause many challenges during arguments, especially when couples don't understand and respect their unique brain wiring.

Let Him Cool Down. Assure Her You'll Be Back.

It is important to allow your spouse to calm down when he or she becomes physiologically charged up in an argument. Don't follow him into the next room and insist on getting one more word in or force him to resolve the issue in the moment. It won't happen. Not only will you push your spouse further into a fight-or-flight mode, but his cortex or thinking brain is not fully available for a calm and caring conversation. And if you pursue your husband or wife for a comforting response, forget it. In the moment, he can't access the part of the brain that will allow him to be soft, gentle, and understanding.

Take a time-out. Because it is of great value for your spouse to be connected to you, tell him you want to take a time-out, but first comfort him. This helps the perception of danger in the relationship not to feel so scary. It helps each of you know that even though you don't see eye to eye, you still value and love each other. Say something like, "I am so mad right now, I need some time to calm down.

Even though we're angry at each other, I love you and care for you and will come back later to talk about this." You are each assured that you still love each other, want to work things out, but are just caught on the low road of an amygdala hijacking.

Allow each of your heart rates to come down. Then return for a more productive conversation. But be careful. If you promised your spouse you would come back and talk about a topic, then make sure you return within a reasonable amount of time. If you don't, you teach him to respond in a way that you won't like. Your spouse will soon realize that a time-out means you are "ducking out," and the next time you request one, he or she will be reluctant to give it to you. Instead he'll follow you in an attempt to be heard right now, knowing that "we will talk about this later" will not come.

BACK TO THE BOX OF CHOCOLATES

Let's take a closer look at the intricate workings of the emotional brain and how it relates to our story at the beginning of this chapter about Randy and Jessica's argument over the box of chocolates.

The Triggering Event

Jessica was at first very excited about the box of chocolates, not only because she enjoys chocolates but because of what it meant about her and Randy's relationship. He was thoughtful and kind, and this was very meaningful. Good-feeling hormones rushed through her body as she got a glimpse of how glad she was to be loved by Randy. Warm thoughts filled her mind.

Her Dragons Raised

When Jessica opened the box of chocolates and looked for her favorites, disappointment hit her like a ton of bricks. Her amygdala jumped into action, asking, "Is the omission of your favorite chocolates dangerous?" Scanning her memory banks, it answered with a resounding yes!

At this point we need to go back and understand a bit of Jessica's background to discover what experiences are stored in her long-term memory banks from growing up that are possibly influencing what she sees as dangerous and how she reacts.

When Jessica was a child, her mother would often make wonderful promises of outings and holidays, saying, "This weekend we are going to the park," or "Tomorrow I will take you to the mall to shop." But inevitably something would happen to prevent Jessica's mother from following through on her promise. Her mother was either too depressed, or too consumed with Jessica's younger brother, who suffered from epilepsy. Jessica would get excited, only to be disappointed. The lens through which she viewed life said, *Eventually the person you love so much will disappoint and hurt you, so don't fully trust.* Jessica is sensitive to rejection, and anything that feels like rejection touches a tender, hurtful, and vulnerable place within her.

Haven Not Feeling So Safe

There was also something happening in Randy and Jessica's relationship at the time that primed her to see everything Randy did through the lens of "you are not there for me." All month Jessica had been feeling lonely and disconnected from Randy. From this emotionally depleted state, she was not able to see Randy as having the right intentions or to put his mistake into the broader context of their relationship and say, *Well, he did get me the chewy nuts. Besides, we have been connected and getting along well tonight, and the omission of the caramels doesn't mean he doesn't consider me.*

Alarms Sound Off

Jessica's amygdala sounds the danger alarms, leaving her feeling hurt, angry, and ready to respond. Her heart beats faster, her blood pressure goes up, and the palms of her hands begin to sweat. She could freeze and say nothing, but she never has and probably wouldn't know how. She could flee, or withdraw, as she did when a little girl, going to her bedroom and crying alone. But as an adult she usually expresses her hurt and disappointment by protesting and angry words. Fighting has become her automatic way of reacting when she feels hurt by Randy.

And because the amygdala has the ability to immediately influence the entire brain and body, before Jessica's thinking brain can reevaluate the situation and recall the handy-dandy communication skills she learned at their last couple's conference, critical remarks roll off her lips: "You are inconsiderate, you don't care about me, and you are selfish."

She responds so strongly because she feels that a gentler, more well-mannered comment wouldn't get through to him and make him understand how wrong he is and how hurt she feels. Anyway, she has told him what she needs before, and he has just ignored it. So since her emotional brain is flooding her thinking brain with negative information stating, "Trust me, this man did not consider you, just like all the other times this month," she feels justified feeling so angry and reacting the way she does. By the time her cortex re-evaluates the situation later that evening, drastic conclusions and hurtful words have already been verbalized.

The Triggering Statement

Now let's see what's going on inside Randy's head. The instant he hears the words "You are selfish" come out of Jessica's mouth, his relationship system evaluates, *Is Jessica my safe haven right now?* The answer is no.

His Dragons Raised

Then his amygdala asks, "Is this a dangerous statement?" and the answer for Randy is yes. The seemingly small word *selfish* hit Randy's hot button dead center, touching the core of his vulnerability. Randy has always prided himself in being fair. He can remember his grand-father sending him five dollars and a note saying, "Your cousins were in town, and I took them out to lunch. This is what I spent on them. It's only fair to send you the same." That taught Randy a lifelong les-son in fairness, which he has tried to practice all his life. Randy also prides himself in working hard to provide for the family. The thought of Jessica's thinking him selfish is hurtful to him.

Randy thinks, *How dare she call me selfish after all I do to share the household load, as well as the many hours I put in at work for the sake of the family?* Randy's amygdala sounds the danger alarms.

His Emotional Brain Sounds the Alarms

Feeling unjustly accused, alone, hurt, and angry, Randy's emo-tional brain gets him ready to react. Typically he fights to defend him-self, and after he feels he can't change Jessica's mind about how wrong and bad she thinks he is, he withdraws and shuts down. So Randy says with a harsh tone of voice, "I picked the chocolates we usually get." In essence he's saying to Jessica, "I am not wrong in forgetting the caramels; you are wrong in being hurt over the lack of caramels."

Stuck in the Spin Cycle of the Argument

Hearing Randy taking no responsibility for being wrong and seeming unmoved by her hurt, Jessica feels she has further evidence that Randy does not consider her. Her safe haven does not feel very safe. She responds by restating her case louder and with sarcasm: "All I ask is for you to think of me once in a while."

Hearing Jessica's sarcastic remarks makes Randy feel further unseen and unappreciated, so his amygdala keeps him fired up, his heart racing and primed for a fight. He continues to defend himself saying, "No, you are being selfish," and then sends his own counter-attack, shouting, "You are impossible to please!" Jessica hears that statement as "Something is wrong with you for being disappointed."

To Jessica, Randy seems far from a loving, considerate husband, and both become flooded with negative thoughts.

Their heart rates go up ten or thirty beats per minute, and adrenaline and stress hormones surge through their bodies. Both are physiologically charged, their skin temperature has gone up, and so has their blood pressure. Both are stuck in their tunnel perspective, feeling miles apart from each other and as though they are on opposite teams, with no chance of ever understanding each other.

They argue as though their relationship and life depend upon the choice of chocolates. But the argument is no longer about chocolates. It is—and always was—about how safe they feel with each other.

Off the Low Road

When the emotional brain hijacks you and keeps negative emotions running through your mind, you are too busy protecting yourself and fighting the enemy to be emotionally available and listen to your spouse. When your heart is racing, your stress hormones are pumping through your veins, and you're ready to fight, flee, or freeze as though facing an angry gorilla, you don't have the state of mind to listen with empathy to what your spouse is trying to get you to understand.

It makes sense, too, that in these moments, arguing partners aren't easily distracted by other cues. If you're faced with what you think is a rattlesnake on a hiking trail, you don't notice the beauty of the acacia trees, nor do you notice that you're hungry. Being easily distracted could cost you a snakebite.

Likewise while in this state you don't pick up the cue that your wife feels dismissed when you defend yourself or that your husband is beginning to feel flooded when you keep yelling. You forget what hurts your partner's heart and, even if you do remember, you don't care very much when you're stuck on the low road. You're oblivious to the possibility that maybe your and your spouse's dragons, vulnerabilities, and fears are what the argument is really about and that what you both long for is not to fight and be attacked, but to be understood and comforted.

But when faced with the critical or defensive statement your spouse has just made, you don't recall all the good times you have had or how close and connected you felt just an hour ago. Nor do you realize that in a day or sooner you will once again have warm feelings toward your spouse. Instead, you are locked into an emotional state, unable to shift your attention unless something really significant can switch your focus or until you sense that the danger is gone.

You're Not as Dangerous as I Thought

When your amygdala no longer senses danger, the alarms are shut off and your amygdala signals your body to stop pumping out stress hormones. One way this occurs is when you gather information that allows you to review the situation and take a second look, seeing that what you thought was dangerous is not that dangerous. The perceived sense of danger leaves, the stress hormones are flushed from your system, and so does the need to fight, flee, or freeze. After sensing that your spouse is no longer dangerous, you are able to shift into a more empathetic or nurturing brain state and from that place talk and share with your spouse with more understanding.

You experience this shift when new information enters your senses that challenges the old dangerous cues, or when your thinking brain is able to review and take a second look at the situation that your emotional brain so quickly concluded was dangerous. This happens when you're on the hiking trail and your son kicks the stick you thought was a rattlesnake. Or after seeing broken bits of plastic all over your dashboard you realize it was your wife's birthday balloon bouquet that popped, not your tire. Or after taking a deep breath you look into your spouse's eyes and realize, *He does love me and is not out to get me.*

When the danger is no longer perceived as dangerous, your amygdala relaxes, reverses the alarms, and begins to calm and relax

your body. *Whew! It's not a rattlesnake, only a stick.* You are then able
to reach for what you thought was dangerous only seconds before:
you pick up the branch and use it as a walking stick on the rest of
your hike, or you perceive your spouse as being once again emotionally available, responsive, and your safe haven.

You're then able to recall all the times your husband has been
there for you, or gain an understanding of your wife's perspective,
making sense of why he or she reacted in what seemed a rejecting
way. Perhaps you see that behind your wife's critical accusations is
a woman who feels alone, abandoned, and desperate to be close.
Or behind your husband's aloof demure is a man who is afraid of
failing or disappointing. Your cortex is able to pull different parts of
your brain together and create states of mind that allow you to be
understanding, empathetic, and willing to view the situation from
the perspective of your spouse. It helps you weigh your opinions
and thoughts alongside your spouse's and choose a way of responding that is in the best interest of the relationship.

The Repair: Resolving the Chocolate Incident

Later that evening Randy and Jessica were able to make sense of
why the box of chocolates sounded off the danger alarm and triggered such powerful negative responses that sent them straight to
the spin cycle of their argument.

It began when Jessica watched Randy close up the box of chocolates and put them back in his briefcase. She did not see an indifferent,
uncaring look on his face, but rather a sad one. Her airtight argument
against him developed a small crack that maybe his heart intent was set
on pleasing her and that even though he did not pick her favorite
caramel chocolates, he possibly still cared for her. As her thinking brain
reevaluated the situation, her amygdala received new information that
possibly the situation was not as dangerous as she had thought earlier.
She felt a tinge of understanding come over her.

Released from the grips of her amygdala and entering into a more nurturing state of mind, Jessica was able to integrate Randy's experience with her own. She turned toward Randy: "I was so hurt tonight. I think the box of chocolates represented more than just chocolates."

"Yeah," Randy answered after sensing Jessica was no longer armed with anger and that he could now risk and be vulnerable as well. "I think this past month has been hard on us both."

Listening and Understanding

Jessica continued edging a little closer to Randy. "The chocolates made me realize how I miss you. I fear you don't care that we're disconnected. The thought of that is terrifying for me. It sent me through the roof."

Hearing Jessica admit that she "went through the roof" was comforting to Randy as he was a bit surprised by her yelling and throwing the box across the table. When she said she missed him and longed to be close, Randy softened. *She is sensitive to disappointment, and tonight she certainly was,* Randy reminded himself. Jessica's vulnerability allowed Randy to lower his weapons, and he felt her expression of loneliness and sadness tug at his heartstrings. Her pain pulled from him understanding and the desire to comfort her. A new cycle began to unfurl: his softening and turning toward Jessica allowed Jessica to continue to share her vulnerability that allowed Randy to risk and share his softer side.

"I hate working overtime like I have," Randy explained, "but if I get this project done right I hope to get a raise, and that will help our family. This month has been hard on me too; I miss you so much. The thought of your seeing me as being selfish is very painful."

Hearing Randy's heart instead of his defensiveness, Jessica softened further. She felt a wave of empathy for him that made her want to comfort him: "I am so proud of you." She continued. "But I need to feel you care about me. I can't go for so long without time together. I need you."

"I need you too," replied Randy. "I'm so sorry I haven't done a better job of finding time to be together. I know this has been hard on you, and I really appreciate all you've done."

"I know you're busy; I understand that, and I don't mind. I know you need to get this done. I just need to know you still care about me and that I am still important to you," Jessica admitted.

"Of course you are. I love you so much. I work so hard for *us*; I hope you know that. You're right, I haven't made an effort to connect with you and I'm sorry. You know what? I'm going first thing tomorrow and buy you a pound of caramels," Randy said as he reached for Jessica and held her in his arms.

When you no longer feel threatened or abandoned by your spouse and sense your spouse is your safe haven, your amygdala shuts off its internal alarm system. Your relationship system finds that all is well in your safe haven and you're able to shift into a more vulnerable, connection-seeking emotional state. When you feel your spouse is not the enemy but someone who truly cares for you, you feel safe enough to lower your weapons (criticism, defensiveness, blame, withdrawing, etc.) and respond in a more understanding and vulnerable manner (share your hurt, listen to each other's perspective, be open to be influenced by each other, and ask for or give comfort).

Your emotions are calm, and you feel safe, loved, and once again in your safe haven.

QUESTIONS AND EXERCISES

To help you become more aware of what happens during your arguments, recall the last time you and your spouse took the "low road" during an argument and answer the following questions:

1. What was the triggering event?
2. How did you perceive your spouse? (For example, did you perceive your spouse as your safe haven, available

and responsive, listening and trying to understand you? Did you feel your spouse was defending him/herself or attacking you?)

3. What dragons were raised?

Here are a few examples:

No on is there for me.

This is unfair.

I'm not in control.

Don't tell me what to do.

I do all the work, and no one helps or appreciates me.

I am right because if I am wrong, then I am bad and rejected.

I am not respected or considered.

You are not a teammate to me.

I have no spiritual covering over me.

I am always taken advantage of.

I feel cornered and pressured.

No one really understands me.

I am not smart or skilled enough.

I am always left out.

I am always competing for your attention.

I am not noticed.

I feel smothered and controlled.

I am not protected or valued.

It is all my fault.

4. When your emotional brain is triggered, how do you feel stress in your body, and how do you react? (For example, your heart rate goes up, your muscles tense, and you either fight, flee, or freeze.)

5. In the middle of an amygdala hijacking, how can you remind yourself of a more productive way of expressing your perspective?

FIVE THE INEFFECTIVE WAYS WE ARGUE

Learn Better Ways to Be Heard and Understood

"NO MATTER WHAT I HAVE PLANNED FOR THE NIGHT, Tracy does what *she* wants," Jake said with a tinge of anger. "It is so hurtful. I don't feel I'm a priority to her."

"I can't always get off work exactly when I want, so sometimes I'm late. He never understands," explained Tracy.

I asked Jake, "What do you do when this happens, Jake? Do you tell her how hurt you feel?"

Jake laughed. "Oh, I tell her how I feel, all right. I guess my amygdala fires up and hijacks my thinking brain. I yell for a few minutes and say things like, 'You live life as an independent woman, and I am sick and tired of it. Stop it, or I am done!'" He looked down toward the floor and sheepishly said, "Then I withdraw. I feel sad inside because nothing ever seems to change. I feel all alone, unimportant to her. I go into my cave."

"What happens for you, Tracy, when Jake yells?" Tracy glanced at Jake, as if to let him know that what she was about to say could sound hurtful to him. "When he is yelling, I feel I can never do anything right. I will never be good enough for him, and I fear he will eventually leave. I guess that's when *my* emotional brain sends out the alarm, alerting me to danger in our relationship. I feel panicked, as though it's the end of our marriage."

"Do you tell him that?" I asked Tracy.

"Well, no," she answered. "I defend myself at first, then I review all he has done wrong. I think what I told him during this last fight was, 'You are always complaining—you only see the negative. I am sick and tired of your negativity.'"

"It seems that the way you each react does not get you what you need from each other," I summarized.

"I know the automatic way I respond is with anger and harshness," said Jake. "I'm learning that it is not the way to get my wife to understand my point. Instead, the way I react pushes her away."

OUR COMPLEX EMOTIONS

Isn't it amazing the way our emotions become so complex and powerful, taking turns and twists in the middle of our arguments? We can be feeling a softer, more vulnerable emotion inside only to express a harsher, more negative emotion. This causes our spouse to fight back and pull away, leaving us hurt and alone instead of comforted and connected. I've found that this breakdown between what we really feel and how we actually respond happens often with couples. As a result, we get the opposite response from the one we wanted. This is how it typically goes:

> You are gone ◗ I miss you ◗ I feel sad, alone ◗ I get angry, critical ◗ You see my anger ◗ You react to my anger with defensiveness ◗ I react to your defensiveness by withdrawing ◗ You react to my withdrawing with blame ◗ We are left hurt and emotionally disconnected.
>
> What I longed for was for you to hear my view, understand my hurt, and help find a solution together.

You learned in chapter 4 how all reactions in our arguments are fueled by emotions, even when we think we're responding with logic. The fact that we feel and express our emotions is not the problem, though. It's what we *do* with our emotions that causes our arguments to go sideways.

What Are Our Emotions?

Emotions are a summation of what we are feeling and thinking, including bodily sensations, thoughts, and a set of corresponding actions. Here is an expanded list of our basic emotions:

Our Basic Emotions

Fear	Disappointment
Anger	Anticipation
Sadness	Hate
Happiness	Courage
Love	Hope
Peace/Contentment	Wonder/Interest
Disgust	Anxiety
Surprise	Feeling of self-worth
Satisfaction of living a meaningful life	

The Motion of Our Emotions

Emotions are part of God's design to help us be useful and productive and to serve a purpose in our lives. Yes, even though we often work hard not to feel our more painful emotions, all emotions serve a necessary function at specific times. They give us information about the world around us, add meaning to our interactions, and tell us how to react. Coming from a Latin word that means *to move*, emotions connect us with how we feel and think and then move us to action, causing us to respond and react in a particular way. Certain emotions within us trigger certain responses, and likewise, when we perceive a certain emotion in someone else, we are moved to respond in a particular way. In other words, when we express a

feeling, we pull from another person an emotion that moves him or
her to respond in a particular way.

The Motion of Our Emotions

How do you typically respond when you feel anger, fear,
love, or disappointment?

_come close	_comfort	_empathize	_protect
_seek out your spouse	_share/talk	_turn toward	_ask for comfort/ care
_show care and concern	_get mad	_be joyous	_self-soothe/ comfort yourself
_withdraw	_freeze	_shut down	_be perplexed
_lean away	_go numb	_try to share	_do nothing
_pray/seek God	_get busy	_distract yourself	_daydream/ fantasize

When we feel hurt, the natural emotional response is to withdraw and protect ourselves or seek comfort and care from someone.
When we see others hurt, we usually have empathy toward their pain
and are moved to respond by helping and comforting them. Anger,
on the other hand, is a protective emotion that often comes as result
of sensing danger or feeling that our boundaries have been violated.
When others sense our anger, they are moved to protect themselves
from that anger, either by withdrawing from us or attacking back.
When we feel afraid and sense danger, our fear causes us to attack
what is dangerous or run away and find protection. Others usually
respond to our fear by wanting to protect and comfort us.

Different Types of Emotions

You may be surprised that our emotional responses are even more complicated than we've discussed in the last few chapters. We might think there's a direct line between what happens to us and what we feel, but that's not the case. We can experience three different *kinds* of emotions: *primary*, *secondary*, and *instrumental*.

When you are hurt by your spouse, the initial emotional response that wells up inside you is called your *primary emotion*. These are your core emotions—the deep-down, pure emotions you feel at first.

Secondary emotions are those that help us defend or cope with our more vulnerable primary emotions. They often obscure our awareness of our primary emotions, causing us to react sometimes in a totally different manner from our primary emotions. For example, if your parents scolded you as a child for feeling disappointed, you probably found it easier to feel angry instead of sad and disappointed. It became too painful to be vulnerable and felt safer to be protective of your heart. Secondary emotions are the emotions of our low road—the harsh, negative emotions that often stem out of our angry protest and anger of hope.

Instrumental emotions are those we use to influence and move someone to react in a particular way. The intent is to manipulate others. For example, Fred gets arrogant, puffs up, and gets angry because his past experiences have shown him that when he does, people listen. Barbara cries in hopes of making her husband back down from his strong position and not argue with her.

Sometimes we are totally unaware of our primary, core emotions. These *unexpanded emotions* are the unacknowledged emotions that have gotten lost in our automatic ways of feeling and responding. When growing up, many people did not benefit from emotionally aware homes. Maybe you were raised by parents who did the best they could with what they had but did not know what to do with your emotions. They didn't help you make sense of what you were feeling by helping you put into words those feelings and inner experiences. They were either *dismissive*, telling you to go to your room until you were done with expressing that emotion (such as anger, sadness, disappointment, frustration), or *scolding*, warning the arrival of a spanking or a time-out if you continued to feel a particular way. Or they *sailed over* your emotions, saying, "Sorry you feel that way," but didn't help you know what to do with your emotions.

When you entered marriage, you brought with you this inability to recognize your emotions. You did not know what your basic primary emotions were or your secondary emotions. And you definitely didn't know what your spouse was feeling. Often, even if you have a sense of what you or your spouse is feeling, you don't know what to do with your or the other's emotions.

Not understanding fully the emotions that lurk beneath your secondary emotions can cause you not to be aware of your own inner world. So if you don't know your primary feelings and only express your secondary emotions, you will frequently not have your primary needs met. It makes sense then that you would also not be very aware of your spouse's inner world and needs. As a result, both you and your spouse are left feeling unseen, unheard, misunderstood, missed, not comforted, and not connected to each other. I'm sure you have heard either yourself, your spouse, or someone else say, "Well, what am I supposed to do with your feeling, anyway?"

Candy Coating—So I Don't Melt in Your Hand

I have often used the image of a candy-coated chocolate to explain emotions. Primary emotions are tender, like the soft chocolate center of a coated candy. The candy coating is like our protective secondary and instrumental emotions, such as the protest and anger of hope you feel when your relationship system senses that your spouse is not there for you. It could also be the negativity you feel when in the grips of the emotional brain's stress/fear response.

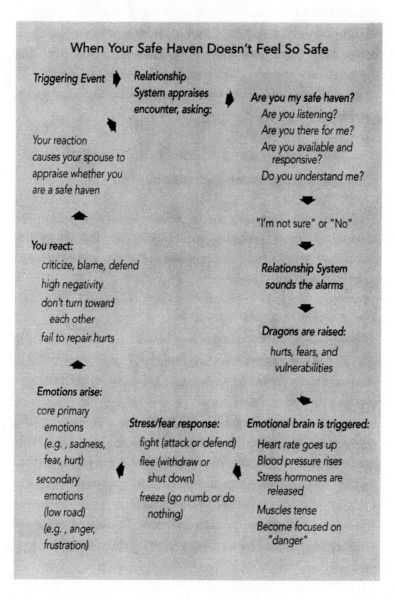

When Your Safe Haven Doesn't Feel So Safe

Triggering Event ▶ Relationship System appraises encounter, asking: ▶ Are you my safe haven?
Are you listening?
Are you there for me?
Are you available and responsive?
Do you understand me?

▼

Your reaction causes your spouse to appraise whether you are a safe haven

"I'm not sure" or "No"

▼

You react:
criticize, blame, defend
high negativity
don't turn toward each other
fail to repair hurts

Relationship System sounds the alarms

▼

Dragons are raised:
hurts, fears, and vulnerabilities

▼

Emotions arise:
core primary emotions (e.g., sadness, fear, hurt)
secondary emotions (low road) (e.g., anger, frustration)

Stress/fear response:
fight (attack or defend)
flee (withdraw or shut down)
freeze (go numb or do nothing)

Emotional brain is triggered:
Heart rate goes up
Blood pressure rises
Stress hormones are released
Muscles tense
Become focused on "danger"

The candy coating of our harsher secondary emotions functions as self-protection to the raw hurt and vulnerability of our primary emotions. So instead of showing you are feeling afraid, you get angry. Instead of constructively expressing your hurt (and honestly, maybe you don't even know how to put your feelings into words) you express angry defensiveness. Instead of showing your sadness, you push away and go numb. Painful emotions such as fear, hurt, and shame are often defended, numbed, or suppressed rather than felt and expressed.

So when you miss your spouse, instead of sharing your sadness, you express:

- your disappointment in his inability to ever be on time and
- your anger at her inconsiderateness.

The breakdown of not sharing primary emotions directly and honestly and instead presenting harsher secondary and instrumental reactions is what derails your arguments. It leaves you both feeling misunderstood and disconnected.

The Spin Cycle of Our Emotions

Imagine with me that you are hurt because your spouse stayed up watching the news later than you had hoped. Now you don't have time to spend together before going to bed. You are hurt, feeling as though your spouse doesn't make you a priority.

Your relationship system sounds the alarms, and your amygdala gets you ready to react. You protest your spouse's poor decision to watch television rather than be with you. *I am not going to be treated and hurt this way*, you find yourself thinking, and your anger (secondary emotion) serves to protest the disconnection, hoping your spouse will realize how hurt you are (primary emotion). The harsher outer coating of anger is a way of protecting yourself from being hurt.

As your wife (or husband) finally climbs into bed ready to snuggle with you, what does she see on your face and hear in your voice? Yes, your anger. And exactly what does she react to? Your anger! Your spouse doesn't see your sadness and desire to be close; all your spouse experiences is your anger.

This brings your wife's relationship system to ask, "Are you listening? Are you there for me? Are you available and responsive? Do you understand me?" Well, let's think about this. The tone of your voice, the look on your face, and the words from your mouth imply no! And as a result, her relationship alarm system is triggered and ready to defend her. Sadly, defensiveness was the last thing you wanted from your wife. And to top it all, her defensiveness adds to your feeling hurt and disconnected.

Let's go back to the primary emotions you were feeling right before you responded with secondary anger: sadness and longing to be close. Now if your wife knew you felt sad because you missed her, she probably would have comforted you. But you didn't express your softer primary emotions, so she never saw your heart. The chart on the next page explains how this complex, powerful negative cycle (as liiustrated below) takes hold of all your arguments.

What Happens in the Spin Cycle?

He is protesting her being late because in the moment he feels she doesn't value him.	▶	She is defending herself against his anger and critical attacks and doesn't see his hurt.
He missed her and really wants her to see his sadness, come close, and problem-solve.	▶	She would be able to comfort him if she knew he was sad and missed her (or he could teach her what he needs to be comforted).

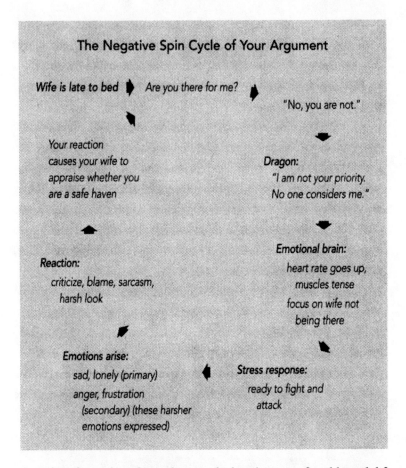

The Negative Spin Cycle of Your Argument

Wife is late to bed ▶ *Are you there for me?* ▶

"No, you are not."

*Your reaction
causes your wife to
appraise whether you
are a safe haven*

Dragon:
*"I am not your priority.
No one considers me."*

Emotional brain:
*heart rate goes up,
muscles tense
focus on wife not
being there*

Reaction:
*criticize, blame, sarcasm,
harsh look*

Emotions arise:
*sad, lonely (primary)
anger, frustration
(secondary) (these harsher
emotions expressed)*

Stress response:
*ready to fight and
attack*

What if you don't know how to deal with uncomfortable and difficult emotions? If you respond to your spouse's primary emotions—the core softer emotions—by dismissing or minimizing them, your spouse will feel very hurt, maybe even angry. It will put your spouse back into the spin cycle of your argument, confirming that she is not heard, or that you are not there for him. This keeps the emotional alarms sounding loud and clear and validates your spouse's relationship dragons and fears. The vicious cycle will continue.

So how do *you* react and relate to your spouse? How do you attempt to express your emotion or get your point across in a way that your spouse will listen and understand? What do you say? How do you say it? What do you do with your emotions? Do you feel desperate, as though nothing you say will get your spouse to slow down and understand your perspective? Do you feel helpless to influence your spouse in the middle of an argument? Do you feel an urgency to go after your spouse and express your view right now?

From the example of the wife coming to bed later than her husband would have liked, it was not how he *felt* but how he *reacted* and what he expressed that ruined their connection when she finally came to bed. If you are in this kind of situation, do you express your more tender primary emotion of disappointment and feeling abandoned, or do you express a more secondary, harsh emotion of anger and irritation? Do you express your hurt in a considerate, constructive manner or in a negative, degrading way?

How Do You React?

Yell, scream	Be emotionally expressive	Shoot your guns
Raise your voice	State your case like a lawyer	Be prickly and tense
Go soft	Formulate a good argument	Become cold and calculated
Can't find words	Use few words	Withdraw and sulk
Talk in monotone	Attack and run	Become cold, businesslike
Micromanage	Don't know what you feel	Freeze 'til it calms down
Fill the void	Lose steam halfway	Attack and keep going
Seek security	Eventually get overwhelmed	Use a matter-of-fact tone
Minimize	Go silent and hopeless	Use condescending tone

The *way you react* sets in motion a negative cycle or interactional pattern that has the power to keep you and your spouse stuck, fired up, and unable to listen to and understand each other. In your attempt to express hurt or to try and get your point across, the way you react can either foster a closer connection or trigger anger and frustration.

So how do you stop this negative cycle? Slow down and take a closer look at not only what makes you upset but also how you react when you are upset. Recognize the impact you have on your spouse. Ask yourself these key questions:

- Do I have to react this way to be heard and understood?

- What am I really trying to get my spouse to understand?

- If I react this way, will I get the comforting response I long for from my spouse?

THE DESTRUCTIVE WAYS COUPLES RESPOND

To give you a better understanding of why you react the way you do, let's look at some research findings about couples, which will help you evaluate the way you react when in the grips of an amygdala hijacking.

Hey! You'd better listen up!

The Harsh Start-Up

The first minute of your argument will determine the direction it will take. When a legitimate complaint, concern, or point is brought up in a harsh manner, an argument will go sideways. Picture with me a husband storming into the kitchen and with an intense tone of voice and stern look on his face saying to his wife, "I told you not to park in front of the garage. Why don't you listen to anything I say?"

Now picture another scene: A wife wants to spend more time with her husband and as he repacks his golf clubs, she starts up, "Why don't you ever want to spend time with me? Your work and golf games are always more important than me. You never make time for us to be together."

Research shows that when a wife presents a complaint with a negative and harsh tone, her husband will respond defensively with the same emotional intensity, and the argument will escalate and end on a negative note. When a spouse raises an issue regarding the couple's "hot topic" in a harsh manner, the other spouse is not interested in talking about his or her day in a later conversation. It's understandable that if your spouse has just jumped on you about something, you feel attacked and not in the mood (or physiological state) to be caring and considerate in return. John Gottman found that 80 percent of the time it is the wife who brings up the tough issues, but in my clinical practice, both husbands and wives long for an emotionally connected relationship and complain when their marriage is not.

The statement "You don't . . . you always . . . you never" will not switch the lightbulb on in your husband's heart and get him to confess: "I am so wrong. You are right. I *don't* want to spend time with you, my work and golf games *are* more important, and I *never* make time for you . . . You are right . . . I am so sorry . . . Let me correct that right now."

Sometimes we feel so strongly about something that our emotions well up inside and harsh words come out before we catch ourselves. When that happens, we need to "back up."

I jumped right in, didn't I? Sorry. Let me first give you a kiss hello, then rephrase what I said in a nicer way.

Instead of Harsh Start-Up, Introduce Complaint Gently

If you find yourself starting a conversation with a harsh start-up, try this three-step repair process:

1. Catch yourself and stop!
2. Apologize and let your spouse know you don't intend to be harsh, just understood. Say, "I am sorry; I was harsh."

3. Ask for a "start-over," or "do-over." Mid-sentence catch
   yourself and say, "Well, that was harsh of me. Sorry, can
   I do it over?" Or, "Let me start this conversation over. I
   am very upset about the fridge breaking down, but I
   don't want to attack you."

Criticism

A criticism is a legitimate complaint with a "What is wrong
with you?" added to it. It is when you have something very constructive to tell your spouse, but you say it in a way that adds
"Something is wrong with you for thinking that, doing that, saying
that!" It implies that your spouse is defective in some way and what
he is doing is a symptom of what is wrong with him. A criticism
can come across as:

- *Warning:* "You are carrying too many things and you're
  going to drop them all. What is wrong with you? You
  should know better."

- *Blaming:* "It's your fault the key broke because I told you
  to be careful when opening the door."

- *Passing judgment:* "Fathers just don't play that rough with
  their kids."

- *Global:* "You always carry too much stuff" or "You are
  never careful."

- *Condescending:* "What are you doing? Is that how you
  think it is done? Well, it is not. Give it to me."

> *Thanks for playing with the kids, but could you not throw the ball inside?*

Instead of Criticizing, Complain Constructively

What can you say when your spouse says something you think is stupid or is doing something that is clearly not going to work? The rule of thumb is this: if you are pointing out a legitimate complaint or concern and you add, "What is wrong with you for doing or thinking that?" then you have cut your spouse down a notch or two, and it will only make him feel belittled and attacked. He will feel as though you are finding his faults and concluding that something is wrong with him. This kind of criticism will not bring about an "ah-ha" moment for your spouse, causing him to say, "Oh yes, something is wrong with me; thank you. How stupid of me to have done it that way! Forgive me. I want to change and do it differently." No, criticism will only trigger defensiveness.

Instead of criticizing, review in your mind exactly what you would like your spouse to understand. What is your legitimate complaint? Rephrase your criticism into a palatable complaint. And since "a spoonful of sugar helps the complaint go down," it might be a good idea to affirm your spouse first, then attach your complaint.

> *I yell?! You should hear yourself yell!*

Defensiveness

Imagine with me: Your wife has just told you that something is wrong with you for putting a wet towel on the bed. When blamed or falsely accused, your immediate reaction is probably to defend yourself. You might not feel you are as bad as she says, so you deny any blame or responsibility. Your focus becomes how innocent and right you are and how wrong she is instead of focusing on understanding your spouse's concern about the wet bed.

Defensiveness comes in many forms, and here are some you may have heard or used yourself:

- *Denial of any responsibility:* "I did not do it." "You're kidding, right? I don't do that." "How could you even think I am that way?" "In my heart of hearts I was not trying to belittle you" (so I can dismiss your feelings and take no responsibility for contributing to your feeling hurt).

- *Explaining yourself or making excuses:* "I know what I am doing." "I was just about to do it." "I have everything under control." "I try hard to come home early from work. I help you with the kids. I can't believe you said that about me."

- *Sending back the same criticism your spouse gave you:* "Well, you think I carry a lot of stuff? You should see what you try to carry." "You think I yell?! You should hear yourself!" "If the situation were reversed, you would be just as upset with me."

Defensiveness is also filled with:

- *Yes-buts:* "Yes, I have a lot of stuff, but you sure don't help me." "Yes, I yell, but I wouldn't have to if you just listened."

- *Innocent victim:* "I didn't mean it the way you are taking it." "What are you complaining about now?" "If that is what you are getting out of what I said, then I will never get you to listen to me." "Can't I just relax for one minute?" "You always have a set of hoops for me to jump through."

- *Lawyer's case:* You bat away the accusation and present your reasons to the contrary: "I am not carrying a lot of stuff; I know what I am doing. I am a careful person; I have everything balanced. How can you accuse me of being careless?"

- *Body language:* Sometimes your defensiveness is said loudest with your body language, such as a curled-up lip, rolling your eyes, folding your arms, or touching the back of your neck with a perplexed look on your face.

Before Defending, Get to the Truth

Help me understand when you say, "I don't spend time with you," because I feel I do. It must hurt if you feel I don't; I want you to feel loved by me.

It is difficult to see your spouse's feelings and perspective when you think you did nothing wrong. Jack admitted, "The minute I hear April say something I disagree with, I bat her complaint out of the ballpark. Actually, I feel insulted and disrespected. How can she even think that about me?" You are quick to try to set your spouse straight, but what is your spouse trying to get you to understand? Is there a piece of truth in what he or she is saying?

Sure, your wife says, "You never spend time with me." But honestly, do you? Instead of acting like an innocent victim of your spouse's drive-by criticism, try taking responsibility for your part. Try to recognize the bit of truth in what your spouse is saying. For example, even if you think you spend more than enough time with your wife, think of what it must be like for her if she feels you don't. It must feel lonely, sad, and hurtful to her. And when you tell her she shouldn't feel sad when she misses you, ouch! It must hurt her more. Try comforting her sadness. (I will explain how in chapter 9.)

Defensiveness does not make your spouse feel heard, understood, or valued. Instead it says, "I don't care what you're trying to tell me, I don't agree with it, I don't want to hear it, and not only am I right, but you are wrong." This does not cause your spouse to "see the light" but rather "see red" and escalate the conflict.

Look who is talking. The way you act, you're the last person to tell me what respect is.

Contempt

When our criticism is received with defensiveness, we are prone to respond with contempt. We see this happening when a spouse feels superior and intentionally seeks to convey disgust toward his or her partner in some way. It gives the impression that "I am more careful, responsible, efficient, productive, and better than you." Gottman says this is the worst way of relating to one's spouse and is the strongest predictor of divorce. The partner who becomes contemptuous feels absolutely right and, drawing from his or her long-simmering negative thoughts about the marriage, has quickly forgotten all the positive qualities of the spouse.

Contempt comes in the form of:

- *Name-calling:* "What an idiot." "You are such a baby. Don't be so clingy and needy." "Give it up, Mr. Fix-it, and call the plumber."

- *Hostile humor, even ridicule:* "Oh yeah, right, like you'd know how to open the jar. That's a good one. Give it here before you make a mess of things."

- *Mockery, put-downs, belittling, demeaning remarks, sarcasm:* "I'd ask for your opinion if I thought you had something to say." "Yeah, right, you on time? Now that is something I would like to see." "No, give the tickets to me; if you keep them, they will get lost like everything else you lose." The strongest impact on a spouse is what John Gottman calls "the look of contempt." The look is when the lip curls (creating a dimple), the eyebrow is raised, and the eyes roll as the spouse exhales. When your spouse gives you "the look," you immediately know danger lies ahead, and your heart rate goes up.

Why would it make sense for someone to respond with contempt? The giver of contempt often feels justified: "Well, if my wife did not do or say what she does and says, then I would not have to respond in this way." Or "I get to this point when my husband keeps defending himself, and I am so frustrated." And "Well, he does act like one of the children sometimes." Those who get stuck expressing contempt feel they have reached a point of total frustration, and contempt is the next logical step in trying to get their point across.

What does it feel like to be the recipient of the above contemptuous comments? It is no surprise that recipients of contempt do not feel understood and definitely not valued. They feel belittled, devalued, unworthy, ridiculed, sad, and hurt. "I feel like dirt when my husband says to me, 'What are you thinking when you say such stupid things as that?!'"

Or "When my wife gives me 'the look,' my heart sinks to the bottom and I think, *Great, I am in big trouble now.* It saddens me and I feel rejected, like the dog thrown out in the cold just for climbing on the couch."

Don't Demean but Value Your Spouse

> *I would like you to be on time more often, but know that I do value your easygoing spirit.*

To stop contempt from being part of your arguments, you will have to take responsibility for your way of reacting and exert much self-control to keep from showing those feelings. State your complaints in kinder terms so your spouse doesn't feel put down or the need to be defensive. What is helpful is to find a list of what you value and appreciate in your spouse, rather than viewing everything he does as wrong, irritating, and not good enough. It is important to work toward accepting the way your wife does things and the speed at which she does them.

Nagging: Repeating some complaint in a critical manner at awkward times

"I am last on your priority list; you never help around the house. Why don't you ever help me?"

Threatening: You are desperate to get your spouse to understand your perspective and change

"Fine, I'll go with you, but see if I smile the whole night."

"I tell you, I don't deserve this; there is someone out there who will value being with me."

Punishment: You seek revenge and hurt your spouse back

"I won't get your dry cleaning." "I won't buy you a present." (an outright act)

"I won't sit next to her. I'll make her hurt like she hurt me." (a subtle punishment)

Sulking: You shut down, grunt your answers, make no eye contact or conversation—a way of getting your spouse to see your hurt or manipulating for change

Negative interpretation: You each interpret the other's intentions as negative:

"You called late because I am not a priority to you."

"You don't help me in the kitchen because you view me as your maid."

"You don't value me; all I am good for around this house is my paycheck."

Withdrawing and Stonewalling

Whatever.

An emotional withdrawal is going silent, sulking, or not reacting at all. Body language is closed, he looks down or away, or closes his eyes and rubs his forehead. Answers of a stonewaller are short, often one syllable, as in "Humph" and "Whatever." A stonewaller shuts out his spouse by turning on the television, picking up the newspaper, or physically leaving the conversation.

When a spouse stonewalls and withdraws, he conveys icy distance, disapproval, and an attitude of "I am sick and tired of hearing you; you are not worth listening to any further." When a husband stonewalls, it often causes his wife to become more aggressively insistent. In her elevated stressful state of mind, she in essence says, "How dare you shut me out! I will come after you to get you back into the conversation." This is a dangerous moment. It's definitely time for a much-needed time-out. Gottman recommends that couples stop arguing the second they realize their heart rate has gone up. You could make a quick check of your pulse, or just stop when you feel your emotions rising and say, "I am too hot and in no shape to have this discussion now. Let me step out for a minute to cool down." The best way to exit an argument is probably to say so, rather than to withdraw by stonewalling.

When an argument has been going on for a while, one partner usually becomes emotionally and physiologically flooded—feeling overwhelmed and drowning. When you're flooded you begin to feel angry, hostile, and helpless about what to do or say. You feel overwhelmed by the negativity of your spouse, trapped, and stuck as though nothing you can say will change your spouse's attack. Your heart rate goes up ten to twenty heartbeats a minute, your breathing becomes shallow, your blood pressure increases, and stress hormones are released. You begin to feel threatened or, as Gottman says, as though in the presence of a feared object. Once your arousal system becomes flooded, you enter the fight-or-flight stress mode. The fight mode leads you to increased criticism, defensiveness, and contempt, but the flight mode leads you to withdrawal. In this physiological state of mind, you can no longer listen to or empathize with your spouse. You hit a wall and are done with the conversation.

Often, in an attempt to avoid feeling flooded, one spouse will stonewall. Stonewallers, 85 percent of whom are men, feel they are clicking into neutral after they have been repeatedly and unjustly bombarded with their spouse's heated emotions. They pull back and shut down to stop the argument from getting ugly. "At that point," one client said, "I feel as though one of us could get aggressive. I am so hurt and so done, I just have to leave. So I get in my car and drive around for hours." Another says, "I am so hurt by what he has said, I don't know what else to say to do. My only option is to walk away, to just remove myself and think."

What does it feel like to suddenly be faced with a stonewall? "I feel desperate when he shuts me out as though he doesn't care for me anymore. I yell, I say mean words, but nothing can penetrate his shell or get through to him. I want any reaction, so I keep going after him. I want something, even if it's an angry response. I just can't have him shut me out like that."

> *Let's take a break for a minute . . .*
> *I need a time-out to cool down.*

Instead of Flooding, Take Time Out to Calm Down and Self-Soothe

Check your heart rate. Put two fingers on your neck, just below your ear. Feel for your pulse. Don't push down too hard. Count the number of beats in a fifteen-second time period. Multiply by four.

That is your heart rate. Don't argue if your heart rate has gone up ten to fifteen beats a minute over your resting state. You will not be a good spokesperson for your perspective if you are fired up in the grip of your amygdala.

Understand that when you or your spouse has become flooded and stonewalls, it is difficult to calm yourself down. The best way to self-soothe is to take a break from the argument. How do you exit an argument that has overheated?

It's best to say, "Love you, care for you, but I need a time-out to cool down. I'll be back." Or "We love each other, but right now we are so mad; let's not make this worse. Give me twenty minutes." And if your spouse puts up the white flag, signaling a time-out, it is best to do the same. Nothing good happens when you are both stuck in the fight-or-flight stress mode. No resolve will be made, no understanding will happen, and no point will be heard.

Doing It Differently

During the first few hours of the Haven of Safety Intensives, I ask couples to explain to me how they argue and what tactics they use. They describe how they try to get their spouses to understand what they feel or think and the consequent pursue-withdraw pattern that follows: chasing the spouse in hopes of grabbing his or her attention while the other is ducking or attempting to slip out of the angry noose. I then ask a simple question that seems to change it all: "After all these years, does the way you try to get your point across work?"

At first they freeze. They pause and think. Well. Mmm. After a few seconds their answer is always, "No, the way I react does not work."

"She still doesn't get how I need her to be more affectionate with me."

"He still doesn't understand why I am hurt by his impatience."

We don't intend to, but we end up hurting each other in our desperate attempts to be understood.

WHAT AM I TRYING TO SAY WHEN I SAY . . .

The greatest gift you can give your marriage is to learn how to share your emotions in constructive and honoring ways. The key to learning how to argue is understanding what you are trying to say to your spouse. What are you feeling under all the criticism and defensiveness, the anger and frustration? What are you really trying to say to your spouse?

The journey begins when you slow down and understand what you are feeling when you get irritated and frustrated. Don't lash out with a blaming statement that will take you down the wrong road: "You don't care," followed by a defensive, "Yes, I do, but you are always mad," followed by a contemptuous, "If you can't love me, I'll be glad to find someone who will," which ends with withdrawing, "Forget it; just leave me alone," only leading to more frustration.

Instead of reacting out of your anger at what you feel is an attack, a false accusation, a slam, or a put-down, share how you are feeling. How do you express what you're feeling in a way that your spouse can hear you and get your point? When you present your perspective in a non-attacking manner, your spouse will be less defensive and probably feel safe to risk and listen. In the following chapters of this book I will give you six principles and doable techniques on arguing effectively and lovingly with your spouse.

QUESTIONS AND EXERCISES

1. Review your last argument. Did you feel disrespected, disappointed, let down, ignored, or other such emotions? Were you able to express them to your spouse, or did you instead express your secondary, harsher emotions?

Your primary emotions	Your secondary
Disappointment, let down,	emotions/reactions
ignored	anger, criticism,
	blame, defensiveness

2. How did you and your spouse react to each other during the argument? Were any of these harsh responses present?

harsh start-up	criticism	defensiveness	contempt
name-calling	hostile humor	put-downs	sarcasm
nagging	threatening	withdrawal and stonewalling	
punishment	sulking	negative interpretation	

3. What were you each feeling under all the criticism, defensiveness, anger, and frustration? What were you really trying to get each other to understand?

4. Do you have to react this way to be heard and understood? What is another way you can react in order for your spouse to listen and understand? Explore other ways you and your spouse can react in order to be heard.

PART TWO

Six Principles for
Arguing So Your
Spouse Will Listen

SIX PRINCIPLE ONE:
CREATE A SAFE PLACE

THINK BACK TO THE LAST TIME YOU AND YOUR SPOUSE GOT caught in the spin cycle of a heated argument. Maybe your spouse said something hurtful, or you felt she was not listening or understanding. Your dragons were raised, your relationship system sounded the alarms, and your emotional brain took over your thinking brain. Your stomach went into a knot, your heart started to pound, and you could feel your palms sweating. Yes, you know what this means (at least after reading this book, you do). You were ready for an argument!

When you are stuck in the grip of your anger, it is difficult to see anything else except your frustration, hurt, irritation, justification, and perspective. If you stay there, your argument will continue to go sideways, and negativity will consume not only the argument but your marriage. That is why it is vitally important to slow down the negativity that flies in the heat of an argument. To change the way you argue, you first must choose to create a safe place for each other.

When you are immersed in your own emotional perspective, it is important to help your emotional brain realize when the danger (such as your spouse's negative comment) has been attended to and is no longer a threat. You could say to your emotional brain, "Yes, I heard my spouse's negative comment, and I can deal with it. I believe we will be able to work this out." In this way, your stress response quietens down. You are then able to enlist another helpful and inti-macy-promoting part of your brain—the part that remembers the positives of your spouse, sees the situation from your spouse's per-spective, feels what your spouse might be feeling, and explores options for a solution and a "we both win" outcome. You are then able to shift from anger, fear, or rage to a more nurturing and caring brain state. This will enable you to:

- see beyond your own tunnel and viewpoint
- understand and hold your own perspective along with your spouse's
- make sense of your own feelings, needs, and hurts, as well as your spouse's
- recall the positives about your relationship and spouse
- explore options and solutions
- respond in a more empathetic and caring manner

Your spouse has the power to hurt and wound you deeply because he or she means so much to you. Although deep inside you know you love your spouse, the heat of your emotional brain taking over pre-vents you from feeling it in the moment. Your dragons tell you ways to fight, retreat, duck, protect, or take cover. When in the middle of an argument, all your negative thoughts and memories regarding your spouse play their PowerPoint presentation.

Chances are that a few hours later, or at the most a few days later, you and your spouse will be back in relationship again, feeling warm and caring toward each other. At the peak of an argument, the good of your spouse and relationship is lost in the midst of the hurt and anger of the moment. You are not thinking about your safe haven, although you should. Whether on the brink of an argument or in the heat of your stress response, don't forget the incredible value of your relationship and the worth of your spouse. If you do, negativity will take root and grow like wild weeds in your relationship.

THE DESTRUCTIVE POWER OF NEGATIVITY

Negativity is a powerful destroyer of a marriage's safe haven. Allowing the negatives, the hurts, and the wrongs of your spouse to roll around in your mind will destroy yours as well. *Rumination* by definition is what cows do when they regurgitate partially digested food in order to chew on it all over again. Bringing back past hurts and negative interactions only to chew on them again is of no value whatsoever. It does not bring about answers or solutions or increase understanding of your spouse. It only solidifies in your brain the negative thoughts and feelings. It actually strengthens the neural pathways connecting the negative situations with your spouse. Your mind holds them, your memory stores them, and when a similar situation arises, the negative thoughts automatically come to mind. Your brain has an incredible ability to keep negative thoughts of your spouse right on the surface of your heart—without your even knowing it.

Couples who are able to think soothing thoughts are able to calm themselves down, say a comforting or soothing statement that disarms their spouse, and pave the way toward making amends.

BE MY SAFE HAVEN

I will never forget when many years ago, Mike, my husband, in the middle of one of our heated arguments, turned to me and said, "Sharon, life is difficult as it is. All I want is to carve out a meaningful life for us where we can support each other, take hold of what God has for us, grow old, and share some happiness together." His words went straight to my heart. Like most couples, we often felt as though we were fighting against each other rather than fighting for more of each other. It's amazing how we end up feeling hurt by the one person we love the most.

As I have heard the same longing in the heart of every couple who enters my counseling room or conferences, I have come to realize that all couples long to carve out a meaningful life with their spouse, where they can support each other, face life's struggles, take hold of what God has for each of them, and share a bit of happiness together.

A powerful way to stop your arguments from spiraling down and preventing your marriage from filling up with negativity is to allow one very positive and powerful thought to challenge the alarms of your emotional brain: *we are each other's safe place.*

OUR ACACIA TREE

I have found the acacia tree to be a meaningful image to visually symbolize the safe place a couple longs to create and live under. As I mentioned in chapter 2, in Africa animals go to find safety and shelter from harm in the shade of the acacia trees. For the animals, the acacia tree becomes a place of safety during the day and rest during the night. The shade and shelter of the acacia tree provide protection in the midst of the battle of life in the wild.

A husband and wife also long to live under the shade and shelter of their own acacia tree. They each leave their single lives to cleave to each other and build a life together, as one. Under the shelter of their marriage relationship, or their acacia tree, they live in the shade of each other. There they become each other's safe place.

Then the LORD God said, "It is not good for the man to be alone. I will make a helper who is right for him" . . . So a man

> will leave his father and mother and be united with his wife, and the two will become one body.
>
> —Genesis 2:18, 24 (NCV)
>
> Yield to obey each other because you respect Christ . . . But each one of you must love his wife as he loves himself, and a wife must respect her husband.
>
> —Ephesians 5:21, 33 (NCV)

OUR ACACIA-TREE PROMISE: WHAT IS TRUE ABOUT "US"

Couples too often argue outside the safety of their acacia tree and lose sight of their safe haven. They forget to remember how much they really mean to each other. In the midst of the struggles of life, affirm the solid foundation of your acacia tree. Through your words, touch, presence, and actions, let each other know that your love for each other will always be there and that you both long to have a safe place.

In your effort to do this, I suggest that you create your own acacia-tree promise—a statement of what you each promise to each other. It would be unmovable and can always be counted on until you and your spouse agree to change it. No matter how hot the arguments get, it is the foundation of "us."

I offer one version of an acacia-tree promise here, but I encourage you and your spouse to either revise it or write your own. Choose phrases and words that reflect your hearts. Make the words simple so that when you argue and feel disconnected and distant, you can remember your acacia-tree promise and be comforted by it.

Let your spouse know that despite all the arguing: "I want to live a meaningful life with you and create a safe haven where we can be there for each other and go through life together as we share in a bit of happiness."

Here are six statements that you might want to include in your promise to each other:

1. We choose to be each other's safe haven.

A husband and wife make a covenant, a promise between God and each other, that they will care for, nurture, love, watch over, respect, honor, and do good for each other until death parts them. If you think about it, when you made your marriage vows, you were actually promising to be a safe haven for each other. That is an awesome task that requires your will, heart, and hard work.

As you and your spouse support and encourage each other through the rough times and the good times, you can choose what kind of haven you will be for each other. Begin by talking about how much you mean to each other and how much you value your relationship. After discussing your commitment to each other, write your first statement, which might look like this:

> **We choose to be each other's safe haven:**
> *Because I love you, I make a covenant with you and God to care for, nurture, love, watch over, respect, honor, and do good for you until death parts us. I will do my part in making our marriage a safe haven for you.*

2. We love each other and want the best for each other.

Aim to make life on earth a bit of heaven for each other. How can you let each other know that you are loved and want the best for each other? What is meaningful to your spouse? What lets each of you feel you are well loved? From working with many couples, here are some suggestions.

A wife longs to feel protected, cherished, and cared for. She needs to experience her husband's cherishing of her in the everyday interactions. Spending time together and sharing hearts connects her to her husband.

A husband longs to be respected, admired, and seen by his wife as "the man," and specifically "her man." Husbands need to know that their wives respect them, are proud of them, value their contributions, and trust their decisions.

Often, sex is important in making a husband feel connected to his wife, although both husbands and wives long to be heard, understood, and valued. Men as well as women long to have someone look into their eyes and say, "I am so proud of you. Look at you—you are wonderful, amazing, strong, and beautiful." Every man who has walked through the doors of my marriage intensives has voiced his deep longing to be valued by his wife.

Couples sometimes forget that they each have a softer side that longs to be loved and respected. Remember: If I don't show you that I love you with my words, my touch, and my actions—how will you ever know?

> **We love each other and want the best for each other:**
> *I love you and I need you. You are very important to me. I want you to know that by how I treat you and react to you—by my words, my body language, my touch, and my actions.*

3. We will face life together as a team, as one, as an "us."

When you and your spouse married, you chose to go through life together; you signed up to be on the same team. Now you are an "us," or a "we." You became partners in life, co-journeyers, and helpmates. Even though you are two individuals, each of your hopes and dreams for life are woven together. And as you go through life as a team, you have each other's best in mind.

When money is tight, you stick with the budget and make sacrifices for the good of the family. When in-laws criticize, you support each other. As I have heard many a wife say, "When my mother-in-law begins to criticize how I raise the kids, I hope my husband will step in and let her know that we have an undivided front. He will stand by and support me, us."

> **We will face life together:**
> *I will always be here to support you, stand by you, and face life together. When life gets difficult, I will be next to you. No matter what, I want the best for you, for us. Because when you win, we win.*

4. We help each other grow as a person.

In the shade of your acacia tree, you each commit to grow as a person, refining your character and becoming more Christlike. We are all on the path of becoming all that God has for us to be. On this journey you and your spouse are growth partners, walking alongside each other as you grow in character.

In what condition will your spouse return to God? Because of being married to you, will your spouse be well loved, well cared for, and nurtured? Are you helping each other grow and become all God has for each of you?

Marriage is not about how happy we can be, but how supportive we can be of each other as we face struggles and grow as individuals. We do not help each other grow by criticizing and pointing out what needs to be changed. But rather, we become agents of change through acceptance, grace, mercy, and kindness in our roles as encouragers, supporters, and helpmates.

> **We help each other become all God has for us:**
> *I want to be part of what God is doing in your life. I want to be your encourager as you become all God has for you. I want you to live life well loved, well cared for, and well nurtured.*

5. We both desire a meaningful and purpose-filled life.

We all long for a life that is meaningful and purpose-filled. We were born with gifts and talents, and using them to their fullest results in a satisfying life. As Eric Liddell, in the movie *Chariots of Fire*, said to his sister about using his athletic ability, "I feel God's pleasure when I run." We team with our spouse not only to seek ways to utilize our gifts, but also to find purpose and direction as a couple and family. We help each other "feel God's pleasure" as we live meaningful lives.

Discuss with your spouse what adds meaning to your life and gives you purpose. Ask such questions as: What do we want to accomplish in the next ten years of our life? What steps can we take to move toward seeing these things happen? What do we want our marriage, or family, to stand for? What impact do we as individuals, a couple, and a family want to have on the world around us? How do we want to be remembered? Finish the statement: "I feel God's pleasure when I (and we) _____."

Out of this discussion, fashion your mission statement as a couple and as a family. This becomes the point on the horizon that keeps you on track, providing direction, hope, and your daily life purpose.

Examples of some mission statements are:

- "We want to be a loving family that values helping others. We want our home to be filled with friends and family and always looking for ways to help others."

- "We want a simple life, valuing the small moments, gathering together family and friends, focusing on relationships, and being together."

We live a life of meaning and purpose, together:

I want to team with you as you grow in your gifts and talents and are used by God. I want us to team together and carve out a life that has meaning and purpose. Together we will live a purpose-filled life and become all God has for us.

6. We share a bit of happiness together.

This sentence might sound simple and rather obvious, but for many couples it is profound. We don't want to be miserable or do things that upset each other. We just want to share a bit of happiness together.

We don't intend to rob each other of our dreams, hobbies, friendships, time alone, ability to succeed, or happiness—although when we are arguing, we feel that is exactly what our spouse is doing. Promise each other that in all your interactions, planning, and arguing, you will remember that you each want a chance at experiencing a little bit of happiness together.

What robs you of your joy? What prevents you from being a contented wife? A fulfilled husband? Talk about those things and make a commitment to enjoy life together; every day find moments when you can "share a bit of happiness together."

> **We find happiness in each other and in life around us:**
> *In the midst of the joys and struggles of life, I want to find happiness with you. I want to enjoy you and find pleasure in the small things of life.*

REMEMBER YOUR SAFE PLACE

Your acacia-tree promise won't keep you from arguing, but it will help you remember your safe place when you're in one of those spin cycles. In those moments, try to remember all that you and your spouse mean to each other. Here are some things to ponder when you're stuck in the heat of the moment:

1. Is this how I will feel about you tomorrow, or is this just what I feel in this moment? It is best that I sift out my legitimate complaints from my generalized anger about you.

2. I must not react out of the anger I feel in the moment; I won't be. able to take back the harsh words. I will only be creating hurts between us. I need to take a deep breath, take a time-out, and slow down my angry emotions.

3. I need to remember your strengths, why I married you, and what is there when the smoke of the argument clears: a person I love and value.

4. If I still have a complaint, then I should ask you to have a discussion outside our argument. I remember that nothing said in the heat of an argument is constructive, no sensible decisions can be made, neither of us is able to hear objectively, have a heart to understand, or have the sensitivity to comfort. I won't keep fighting when each of our emotional brains has taken over.

5. I don't have to react this way to be understood by you. There is another way I can tell you what I am feeling. This is not it. I do not need to criticize, name-call, blame, or be contemptuous to be heard.

6. If you won't listen to me, I need to find another way to communicate with you. Maybe take a time-out for things to cool down. Maybe write a note. Maybe do an activity that could help bring us back together so we can talk about the issue at hand. Maybe I could make a nice dinner, and then we could talk about things over coffee.

You Are More Important to Me

In the middle of an argument realize this: *We are just two human beings struggling to go through life the best way we can. We just want to love and be loved.* When you remember this truth, you are both able to stop and say, *I don't want to end up disconnected for the night, and the dishes are not more important than my relationship with you. Even though we disagree on this topic, I value you, and I want to live life in the shade of our acacia tree and grow old with you as we share a bit of happiness.*

Our Acacia-Tree Promise
We choose to be each other's safe place.
We love each other and want the best for each other.
We are committed to "us."
We are helping each other become all God has for us.
We both want to live a meaningful and purpose-filled life.
We want to experience a bit of happiness together.

QUESTIONS AND EXERCISES

1. List the positive aspects of your spouse. Write these on a card and carry them in your wallet or place them on your bathroom mirror. Refer to them as a reminder of all you value in your spouse the next time you are stuck in an argument and can only remember your spouse's weaknesses.

2. With your spouse, create your own acacia-tree promise statement. Refer to the six statements in this chapter as a reference as you write your own.

3. When stuck arguing, what are the negative thoughts that come to mind about your spouse and/or yourself? Are they legitimate? What positive thoughts can replace them?

SEVEN PRINCIPLE TWO: SOFTEN REACTIONS AND COMFORT DRAGONS

TANNER WAS GETTING ANGRY, AND YOU COULD HEAR IT IN his tone of voice. "I did not belittle you, Cara. I remember what I said, and it was not demeaning in any way. We were just talking."

Cara looked at me and said, "This happens often. What am I supposed to do with my hurt when he doesn't feel he hurt me?"

"Fine, okay," Tanner said in desperation. "I hurt you. Happy? Now what do you want me to do?"

"I don't know," answered Cara.

They both looked at me.

Many couples come to this place, not knowing what to do with each other's dragons and hurts. The answer is simple, but it stumps most couples.

"What would it be like if Tanner touched your face and said, 'It must hurt to feel belittled. I value you and did not intend for you to feel that way'?"

"Wow! That would be incredible. I would probably melt," Cara said, as tears ran down her cheeks and a smile broke out on her face.

"Yeah?" Tanner asked in disbelief. I knew he was wondering if such a simple act would have the power to calm his angry wife. But he would soon realize that if he practiced it enough, he would discover the soothing power of comforting his wife's dragons.

What calms and soothes the hurt and anger of our dragons? Comfort.

Ignoring, minimizing, or invalidating your spouse's emotion will definitely not calm his or her fear, hurt, or dragon. When your spouse expresses hurt and you respond by saying, "That is ridiculous; I don't see why you are hurt," your spouse's relationship system will sound off the danger alarms. It will possibly confirm his or her dragon that you are uncaring.

But to you it feels overwhelming, almost dangerous, to walk toward the hurt of your spouse. You may wonder, *Won't I just get yelled at and clobbered if I go close to my spouse's dragon?*

STEPS FOR COMFORTING HURTS, VULNERABILITIES, AND DRAGONS

I know it is hard to believe, but by understanding your spouse's pain and perspective and offering comfort, you can soothe the hurt and dragons. First, remind yourself of the things that trigger your arguments. I'll refresh your memory.

Dragons

You already know that arguments often begin because you or your spouse has touched a dragon (an inner place of vulnerability), causing a negative reaction. Your dragons trigger a feeling of being shamed, embarrassed, ridiculed, unseen, not valued, pushed, or invisible. As a result you or your spouse feels hurt, anxious, angry, or fearful.

Do you know what your spouse's dragons (his or her vulnerabilities, hurts, fears, and sensitive spots) are? What are yours? If you need to, go back to chapter 3 and list your dragons.

My spouse's dragons are: _____

_____

My dragons are: _____

_____

Personality Differences

Arguments that arise as a result of personality differences can touch many sensitive places and cause many hurts. This happens when, for example, a "go-getter" type of person gets irritated at the slow-acting, indecisive personality of his spouse, making her feel criticized and unaccepted. Or a thinking and more philosophical person points out the downside to his wife's suggestion, who feels her excitement is squelched. Or the fun-loving person is once again late after promising to be on time, which makes the spouse feel unvalued and disrespected. Or a goal-oriented person steamrolls toward her goal in an abrupt and insensitive manner, causing her husband to feel hurt and unimportant.

Daniel, an introvert, feels uncomfortable when his wife, an extrovert, wants to be the first one to a dinner party and the last one to leave. He, on the other hand, prefers to be sociably late and one of the first to leave. It can make Daniel feel pushed, controlled, and manipulated when his wife strongly states that she wants to stay at the party longer.

How would you describe your personality? _____

_____

How would you describe your spouse's personality? _____

_____

How do you and your spouse's personality differences cause friction?

_____

Lifestyle Preferences

Arguments are also triggered as a result of two conflicting life-style preferences, such as those related to money and spending. For example, you want to save every penny you can and feel repainting the kids' bedrooms is a waste of money. Naturally, your spouse views it differently. You feel your spouse is not a team player when she tells you she already bought the paint.

Other conflicts occur over what you like to do for entertainment: Kelly angrily said to a very hurt Anthony, "I was disappointed about our date night last night. I was hoping we would go have fun, like see a play or go bowling. Although the movie was good, I did not want to sit in a dark theater not talking."

What are your lifestyle preferences? _____

_____

What are your spouse's lifestyle preferences? _____

_____

When do you and your spouse's lifestyle preferences cause friction?

_____

HOW TO COMFORT YOUR SPOUSE'S DRAGONS AND HURTS

In South African folklore there's a story of an old, harmless lion who would sit on his mound and roar with all his might. This would scare the other animals and cause them to run away from the roar into the bush. To their surprise, though, the lionesses would be waiting in the thick grass, ready to attack the fleeing animals.

Go to the Roar

Running from the growl could get you into . . . well . . . a bigger mess. The moral? Go to the roar. But how do you comfort an angry and attacking lion? It is not instinctual to go to the roar of a lion, but in your marriage, going toward your hurting spouse to offer comfort is actually very powerful.

When someone is hurt and mad at us, our instinct is to want to either fight or run. But instead of attacking or fleeing, if you put your weapons down and move toward your spouse in an effort to gain understanding and offer comfort, you'll somehow remove the sting from the dragon's flames.

When your wife's dragons rise, lean toward her, put your arm around her, and say, "I care for you. I don't want you to feel neglected (or alone or not valued). Maybe we can work together on finding a solution. I want this to be a win-win for both of us."

Or when your husband's dragons are raised, turn toward him and say, "I value you and respect you. I know we disagree on this issue, but I want to be your teammate and find a resolution—a way that we can both come out happy and winning." Here's an example:

Your spouse: "You left the garage door open last night. Now the rainwater and leaves are everywhere."

Your dragon reaction: "You could have checked the garage last night before going to bed. Why do you always have to put everything on me?"

Your comforting response: "That must be frustrating since you just cleaned the garage. It's very disappointing, I am sure. Let's talk about how the garage door gets closed each night to prevent this from happening."

You Don't Have to Roar Like That to Be Heard

When your dragons are raised, take a deep breath. Your emotional brain is probably on its way to hijacking your thinking brain. And you know what that means: you will soon enter the fight-or-flight stress-response zone, causing your heart rate to go up and your perspective to narrow, which will impair your ability to be objective. Unless you can sift out your softer emotions and legitimate complaint from the hurt of your dragon and choose a different way of expressing your hurt, you will find yourself feeling upset and angry—and probably responding in a critical, defensive, and possibly contemptuous manner. Then you know what will happen next: an argument will start. Since your dragons will take the lead in your argument, nothing productive will come out of it. You will be left feeling hurt and unheard, and your spouse will feel angry and misunderstood. The argument will end with the two of you turning away from each other and disconnected.

If you want your spouse to come toward your roar (your hurting heart), you have to change the way you roar. Then, if your spouse does come close, soften.

Before entering the spin cycle of your argument, take a deep breath, allowing the oxygen to enter your body and brain. This will make way for new thoughts and feelings to enter into your mind and heart.

1. During this time, reflect on the following questions:

   - "What hurt me and caused me to have this strong reaction?"

   - "What am I feeling right now besides angry, frustrated, and irritated?"

   - "What exactly do I want my spouse to understand?"

   - "What do I want my spouse to know about my feelings and perspective?"

If you need to, write down your thoughts to help guide you in your conversation with your spouse.

2. If you want your spouse to come to the roar of your hurt and comfort you, then you need to be aware of the way you roar:

   - "Do I have a critical or angry way about myself when my dragons are raised?"

   - "Am I hurtful with my words when I react?"

   - "Am I defensive, blaming, feeling like a victim, allowing every perspective besides my own to slide off me like an egg on a well-greased pan?"

   - "Is my mood silent but powerfully controlling as I sulk, pout, and withdraw my affection?"

   - "Do I allow my hurt to build up and at unexpected moments trickle out as digs, sarcasm, or silent stubbornness?"

3. What impact does your roar and presentation have on your spouse? Does it hurt? Discourage? Raise his or her dragons?

4. What response do you get? Anger? Frustration? Withdrawal? Make a note to yourself: *When I react negatively, my spouse does not hear my heart, and I do not get the response I long for.*

Listen to Your Spouse

Allow your spouse to tell you his or her hurt. Listen, even if you disagree, even if you feel your spouse heard you wrong and shouldn't be hurt by what you said. Even if your spouse gets the facts and the sequence of events wrong, listen. Listening doesn't mean you agree, are confessing to doing wrong, or are prepared to be the guilty party.

You are only listening and understanding your spouse's perspective. Here's how it might play out:

Your spouse's hurt: .

"You totally ignored me when you marched on ahead of me. You forgot about me and just walked on ahead."

Your defensive perspective:

"No I did not; you lagged behind. I meant nothing by it."

What hurt or which dragon is raised:

Your spouse: sensitive to being ignored, left out

You: sensitive to being told you have done wrong

Dragon fight:

Your spouse protests the disconnection while you attempt to protect yourself from being unfairly blamed. While you each protest and protect yourselves, you enter the spin cycle of your argument.

What listening sounds like:

"Oh, really." "Mmm." "Yeah, that's difficult." "Wow." Your words and body language tell your spouse you are listening. Short words and sentences in response convey that you are listening and not thinking of what you will say in defense.

See if There Is Truth in What Your Spouse Said

Is there any truth to what your spouse is saying? If you look at the situation through the lens of your spouse's eyes, does what he says make sense? A little bit of sense?

Understand what you possibly did that raised his dragons. Was it your tone of voice? The choice of words? Your omission of something? Understand the impact of your action or reaction. Imagine the dragon, fear, hurt, or frustration it raised in your spouse.

For example, Randy asked Nancy to find the previous year's taxes stored in a box in the garage. When she returned, she was frustrated and angry and said, "The garage is a mess; I can't find a thing. Let's just organize the boxes right now." Irritated, Randy answered, "Don't panic on me; I am trying to finish the taxes right now." Nancy went on to tell Randy that the house was a mess and nothing ever got done. Not knowing what to do, Randy picked up the files and left for his office.

What could have been done differently? First, Nancy needed to slow herself down and realize that the sight of mess and clutter makes her feel overwhelmed. Instead of blaming Randy, she should have expressed her softer emotion: "I feel overwhelmed when I see how many boxes we have to sort out; it feels impossible, and I panic." He then could comfort her frustration. "Yes, you do much better when your external world is organized. Maybe we can sit down and come up with a plan to get started on rearranging the garage. But right now, can you get me the files?"

You could defensively say that you don't want to comfort your spouse's hurt when you had nothing to do with it. You might ask: Why should I have to keep putting up with his dragons? *The answer to this question is important: your spouse's dragons are your problems because you married your spouse.* You are partners in life. You walk alongside each other as you grow and mature. Marry someone else and your new spouse will just have different dragons—we all have hurts, vulnerabilities, and soft spots. Marriage is the most intimate relationship where these are exposed and stepped on, but also soothed and healed.

Go Soft and Tell Your Spouse You Recognize His/Her Hurt

You may not agree with why your spouse is hurt and you might feel that he or she is all worked up for nothing. Just let your spouse know that you are genuinely listening and tune in to the feelings:

What does your spouse feel when his/her dragon is raised?

____ ignored	____ let down
____ forgotten	____ disrespected
____ pushed out	____ devalued
____ treated unfairly	____ unfairly accused

These are some of the softer, primary emotions of a spouse who gets angry, critical, and pursues:

___ fear of rejection, abandonment
___ hurt, displayed as anger or frustration/aggression
___ panic ___ desperation ___ loneliness ___ exhaustion
___ worthlessness ___ unloved ___ anxiety ___ insecurity

Some of the gentle, primary emotions of a spouse who freezes, shuts down, or withdraws are:

___ fear of being inadequate ___ helplessness ___ loneliness
___ powerlessness ___ confusion ___ incompetence
___ failure ___ shame ___ overwhelmed ___ suffocation

Offer Warm, Caring Empathy

In light of what your spouse feels and after looking at the above list, how do *you* think it would feel to have those emotions?

___ hurtful ___ upsetting ___ wounded, hopeless
___ sad, gloomy, unhappy ___ distressing, disappointing

Let your spouse know:

"It must hurt to feel alone, abandoned (or ignored, let down, not valued) . . ."

Here's how you might say it:

"I know you got really angry to find out that I'm going on a business trip. I can understand you feel abandoned. It must hurt to feel alone and abandoned."

Comfort

In order to comfort your spouse effectively, it comes in handy to know his or her "love language." What expression of love is most meaningful to your spouse? What makes him or her feel heard, understood, valued, and that you really do care? Is it words of comfort, a warm touch, a kind act, an apology, sitting close and listening attentively, a look on your face, a meaningful conversation, time together? When you discover your spouse's hurt—the soft, tender center of your spouse's heart that needs to be understood and comforted—*comfort* that tender part in a way that is meaningful to your spouse: *I do love you and don't want you to feel abandoned by me. Here, let me give you a hug. You're important to me.*

Express Physical Comfort

Touch your spouse's face. Hold his hand. Caress her back. Sit close. If your spouse needs some time to cool down and regroup before feeling safe enough for physical contact, respect that. Allow this time. If the time away seems to be used for sulking, ruminating, or stewing, then say something. Otherwise, allow your spouse time and then later turn toward each other in a meaningful way.

If physical touch is difficult for you after an argument, request the time to regroup, but always come back within a reasonable amount of time to reconnect with each other. Work hard not to sulk or stew in your time away; it will only strengthen your case against your spouse and justify your disconnection.

Teach Your Spouse What You Need . . . Then Absorb It

Teach your spouse how to comfort you. Be kind and respectful with your words. Don't scold your spouse for not knowing what to do to comfort you, or if he forgets and keeps forgetting what you need. Don't expect him to read your mind and know what you need to feel close. Tell him.

Now, this might look and feel awkward, clumsy, and not from an ideal romantic movie. When your spouse does reach out for you, receive it. Don't criticize the attempt and say something like, "Oh, yeah, and a tap on the back is supposed to soothe my hurt? Well, it doesn't." Rather, teach your spouse what you need. Say, "I appreciate the pat on the back, but a nice, big, warm hug right now would be really nice." Or, "I know you feel connected to me when we hug after an argument, but right now I need to just regroup and have time alone."

Allow your spouse to give you what you need and long for. Let it be a win-win situation. You know what you want, and your husband wants to make you happy. So tell him and then allow him to do it. Even though you had to ask for it, go ahead and receive it. Allow it to reach your heart.

Comforting the Dragons

Joshua and Brittany's story is an example of how dragons can be raised quickly—and how to lower them by offering comfort. Their argument goes something like this:

Brittany: "I have raised your son, Ryan, ever since he was six years old. I don't think he values all I have done for him."

Joshua: "Of course he does. What are you talking about?"

Brittany: "He never says he loves me. I always say it to him."

Joshua: "Oh, come on. You're not going to start on this, are you? He is a high-school boy! What do you expect?"

Brittany: "You always defend him. He gets away with too much in this house. And it is because of you."

Joshua: "How is this all my fault? I don't believe you. Do you always find something to be upset about?"

Here are my suggestions to them as an illustration to help you get better results in a similar argument:

1. Go to the roar. Turn toward your spouse and try to make sense of what is underneath her protest and "anger of hope."

   Joshua: "You seem really angry; what is going on?"

2. Your wife tells you the pain of her dragon.

   Brittany: "I have raised Ryan since he was six, but I wonder if he appreciates me."

3. Just listen; maybe reflect back what you hear her saying. It will invite her to talk more. Nod your head, keep eye contact, maybe say a word, don't look bored or give a glare that says, "Oh, not this topic again." Let her know you are listening and care.

   Joshua: "Yeah, you really want to know if he appreciates all you do."

   Brittany: "Yes, I have put a lot into his life. When he never says, 'Thanks' or 'I love you,' it hurts to think he doesn't value all I've done."

4. What truth is there in what she is saying?

   Joshua (thinks to himself): *Ryan doesn't express his emotions much. It doesn't bother me that he doesn't tell me he loves me, but I see how it hurts Brittany. Maybe I haven't taught the kids how to show appreciation to their mom and stepmother. Maybe I could show Brittany how much I appreciate her as a stepmother to my son.*

5. Express empathy and understanding for what your spouse might be feeling.

   Joshua: "Yes. Hmm. Wow, that must be disappointing. I

know you get frustrated at Ryan, but I guess you feel very hurt by him. It breaks your heart, doesn't it? Blended families are tough."

6. Usually just being heard and comforted calms the dragon and hurt. Often it opens up options, possibilities, and solutions.

Brittany: "Yeah, it is tough. I guess parenting has its ups and downs. But Ryan is a good kid, and I'm glad I have him in my life."

7. Offer your help.

Joshua: "I know you are. I'm glad you're in his life as well. Anything I can do to help the situation?"

Brittany: "Yeah, maybe in front of him you could tell me 'thank you' for things I do."

Joshua: "Sure, I can do that."

QUESTIONS AND EXERCISES

1. Recall the last incident when the roar of your dragon scared off your spouse. How did you react? How did your spouse react to you?

2. How can you soften your reactions when stuck in an argument?

3. What is your spouse's love language? What makes him or her feel comforted and connected to you during and after an argument (meaningful touch, words of affirmation, acts of kindness, gifts, quality time)?

4. What is your love language? What makes you feel comforted, connected, and close to your spouse during and after an argument? What hinders you from absorbing your spouse's comfort after an argument?

EIGHT PRINCIPLE THREE: TALK, LISTEN, AND UNDERSTAND

WHAT DO YOU REALLY WANT YOUR SPOUSE TO UNDERSTAND when you argue? Is it how mad you are? How wrong he or she is? Or something deeper about your heart?

> Jan (yelling from the kitchen): "Can you help me with this?"
>
> Doug (still playing his video game, yelling back to Jan): "What?"
>
> Jan (slamming the kitchen cabinet door): "Never mind."
>
> Doug (realizing trouble brews in the kitchen): "What is wrong with you? What do you want?"
>
> Jan (with anger): "I don't want a husband who is just like one of the kids."
>
> Doug: "I got up from the couch for you to scold me? Forget this."

ARGUMENTS AS AN UNFOLDING CONVERSATION

Marriage would be so much easier if, going into a conversation, we knew exactly what we wanted our spouse to understand. Our requests would be clear, our complaints known, and our feelings sorted out and ready to be shared. All we then would need is a slot of time and a listening ear.

But like many couples in the middle of an argument, you get stuck in the tunnel of your own narrow perspective, hot emotions, and negative interpretation of the situation. Your anger gets mixed in with your hurt, dragons, and fears along with your needs and longings.

Oh sure, you feel angry about what your spouse did or hurt by what he said, or you know you disagree with what she is implying about you. But there is more to your experience than your anger and frustration—more than what your tunnel allows you to see. And like most couples, you don't even know it.

During the process of an argument, you and your spouse could enter into a *discovery conversation* in which your narrow tunnels begin to expand. Your thoughts, feelings, and emotions are explored and sorted through while you listen to and consider each other's perspective. The back-and-forth flow of information, understanding, and concern allows each of your experiences to be expanded and put together in a way that represents a fuller experience outside the tunnel.

When couples talk and unfold their experiences, they come to understand different things about themselves and each other. What they thought they felt at the beginning of the argument was only a part of their whole experience. During dialogue they are able to discover much more about each other than just arguing their angry case.

"As we talk about this, I realize I am hurt by your going on your own, even though I originally said it was fine for you to do that."

"I have been grumpy, I know. And I don't want to put a damper on your excitement. Yes, I am proud of your getting the promotion, but I guess I've been struggling between how much time it will take you away from home and what a great thing this is for your career."

You begin feeling one emotion, which leads you to feel another, and when you dialogue about it, the meaning unfolds and you begin to make connections with your other emotions: your needs, past experiences, dragons, fears, frustrations, hurts, and preferences. During your dialogue you and your spouse put together the different pieces.

The goal of a discovery conversation is exactly as it sounds. It's a conversation that allows each of you to expand your emotional experience, move forward, and discover a richer awareness of yourselves and your situation. You each open up to the other's way of viewing the situation, hold the other's view in balance with your own, allow yourself to be influenced by each other, explore what you each feel, and together discover the full picture of your situation.

DISCOVERY CONVERSATION: DISCOVERING WHAT YOU REALLY WANT YOUR SPOUSE TO UNDERSTAND

The following are some important things to remember as you begin your discovery conversation:

1. Know when your emotional brain has hijacked your thinking brain and your dragons have been raised. Realize that when they are, you react from the limited view of your tunnel.

   Recognize the situations that trigger your dragons and how you typically react when your dragons are raised. From this place, realize you are looking at the situation through the windows of your tunnel, with a narrow and limited view.

   To illustrate, let's follow Ray and Joann as they talk about a hot topic in their marriage: Joann's twenty-three-year-old son, Frank. This argument started when Ray did not want his stepson to borrow the stepladder because Frank did not pack away the lawn mower he used a month ago. Ray got very mad.

Joann: "I know I might be reacting from my own limited view. But this is very important to me, and I feel very strongly about it."

Ray: "Well, I don't think I am viewing this from my tunnel. I think I am right-on about this situation."

Joann: "The mere fact that you can't see your tunnel view says that you are in your tunnel . . ."

Ray: "You are right!"

2. Make it safe for each other to listen and talk.

Become emotionally available to each other. When you are *not* criticizing, blaming, name-calling, reviewing the past, listing examples of why you are right, defending, or withdrawing, you have a better chance of getting your spouse to understand your perspective. Let your spouse know you are open and willing to enter a discovery conversation. Make it safe for each of you to open up and explore your vulnerabilities. Be aware of your tone of voice (lower, slower, softer) and body language. Lean toward your spouse, touch while talking, smile once in a while, nod your head, and let your spouse know you are truly attempting to understand.

3. Expand your experience. Understand what you feel besides angry, shut down, and frustrated.

In the beginning of an argument, your emotional brain probably has you in its grip. You are feeling hot and ready to fight. Your emotions are probably defensive and crusty. Remember, secondary emotions protect your softer emotions from being exposed and your heart from being wounded. Anger covers your fear, sadness, inadequacy, and hurt. Aloofness covers your pain. Bossiness covers your lack of control. Numbness covers your sense of shame. Indifference covers your sense of failure or hurt. Withdrawal covers your sense of helplessness and not being good enough.

When you are not able to slice thin your emotions and identify what you are feeling, your emotions get lumped into large categories. You might be angry, but there are many feelings that get lumped into the one emotion of anger. When angry you might really be feeling misunderstood, irritated, annoyed, forgotten, unseen, ignored, disrespected, or unvalued. Finding the specific emotion you feel will help you understand what is really going on inside of you, what you need, and how to respond. It will also help others know how to respond and comfort you better.

What You and Your Spouse Are Probably Feeling

Some softer feelings *pursuers* have other than anger: rejected, abandoned, alone, worthless, desperate, lonely, unsupported, tired, unlovable, anxious, insecure, misunderstood, desperate to be heard

Some softer feelings *withdrawers* have other than frustration: overwhelmed, suffocated, helpless, powerless, confused, incompetent, not good enough, a failure, always fall short, ashamed, fear of being inadequate

---

For example, you feel angry when your spouse tells you not to be so harsh with your daughter, but when you slice your anger thinner, you discover that you actually feel attacked and inadequate as a mother. Feeling inadequate causes you to feel sad and moves you toward seeking comfort. Then it might also move you to look for some good resources to encourage you as you raise your teenage daughter.

At various times during your argument, slow your emotions down. Take a deep breath and think of what else you could be feeling besides anger, frustration, or irritation. Ask yourself what purpose these protective emotions are serving right now. How can you slow down in order to understand what else you are feeling?

Joann: "If I think of what else I feel besides anger, well . . .
let me see. I was angry at you, Ray, for being so harsh
with Frank. You are a good stepfather to Frank . . .
but I feel you are too harsh with him. I guess I get
angry because I feel I have to protect Frank from your
unfair rules."

4. Share what you are feeling; listen to your spouse.

Focus on the goal of the conversation. To get out of the tunnel, discover a broader view of the other's experience and be impacted by each other's view of the situation. This is for the purpose of gaining understanding of each other.

To share what you are feeling and listen to your spouse, keep your weapons down and stay emotionally connected. There is much give and take, being sensitive, and rephrasing to get through the heated topic toward a deeper understanding of each other. If you feel you or your spouse is attacking or shutting down, slow down. If one gets critical or says something the other doesn't agree with, say so, but keep focused on the topic. Don't get sidetracked. Don't start talking about examples of what happened a few years ago.

Save that for another conversation and stay on this topic. Be willing to let go of the hurt you feel from the words your spouse might use to get a point across, for the sake of the overall goal of understanding each other's perspective.

Joann: "Frank doesn't have a father."

Ray: "What? Then what am I to your son?"

Joann: "You are his stepdad, and both he and I value that. You know what I mean. His real dad has never been around. Don't get so sensitive about it right now."

Ray: "Okay, fine. I'm trying to help him grow up and be a man! He needs to learn responsibility. I'm the only one around here who is doing that. Ever since we married, and he was . . ."

Joann: "Yes, but let's not get sidetracked, Ray."

Ray: "Fine. Okay, back to Frank and today. You seem to give in to him so often. It just angers me when you do. When you give in to him with no consequences, it is just hurting him as a man. What is going on with that?"

Joann: "It sounds like you are attacking me. This is a very sensitive issue for me. Can you be gentler?"

Ray: "Okay, sorry. I just get so mad. All right. Go back and tell me what you feel about Frank."

5. Express understanding and empathy for your spouse's feelings and experience, even if you disagree. An atmosphere of exploration, understanding, and nonjudgment allows your spouse to keep exploring.

Joann: "Hmm. I guess I feel responsible for Frank's happiness. Out of all my kids, he suffered the most when his father and I divorced. He understood what was going on, and I know it hurt him. He has struggled ever since."

Ray: "I know it was a rough season for you and your kids. I know you feel you're the only one there for him, and that's hard for you. I've always sensed your struggle between being loving to him and setting boundaries."

Joann: "Yes, but I want Frank to grow up. I just feel so torn between my guilt, making him happy, and what is really best for him."

Ray: "Yes, and I want to be here for you as you try to do what is best for Frank."

6. Solutions often naturally arise when you feel heard, safe, and connected.

Joann: "I guess if you talk to me first about drawing the line, then I will feel less fearful. I need to trust that you're making a rule because you really do care and want to work alongside me to do what is best for him, and not just because you feel he is irresponsible."

Ray: "Of course I want what is best for Frank. But I can understand how difficult this is for you. Yeah, I can do that."

LISTEN

Sometimes we just need to listen to each other. A good listening ear helps us when we need to:

Vent. We want to get the frustration and emotions out. Just telling someone how rude the bus driver was is all we might need. Once it is out, the anger and frustration evaporate: spoken, heard, and gone.

Think out loud. Sometimes we need to process what happened in an attempt to make sense of it and know what to do next. For many, talking helps them clarify and sort through what they are thinking and feeling. They may start out angry or frustrated and, through the course of the conversation, sort out and make sense of the situation. Sometimes they stray from the topic and repeat themselves. When that happens, just have patience and help your spouse come back to the original topic.

Share and be heard by someone who cares. Most of the time, sharing what we are feeling with someone who will listen, understand, and offer care and comfort is very meaningful. We feel seen, heard, and not alone.

Get input. There are times when we want our spouse's input or perspective on a situation. We hope to hear not their judgment or opinions but their objective thoughts about what might be the best thing for us in this situation.

We need our spouse to know how to listen in all of these ways at different times. For example, your boss is repeatedly critical and becomes defensive when you try to talk to him. There are times when you might just want to vent about a particular bad day with the boss. Sometimes you may need to "think out loud" and process a particularly bad staff meeting. Other times you might want to share your hurt, knowing your spouse will just listen and comfort. Then there are the rare times when you want to sit down with your spouse and say, "How do you think I should approach my boss at the next board meeting when he gets critical of my division?"

Most times, though, all we need is to listen to each other with our full attention and a caring attitude. Listening to each other enables us to:

- clarify our situation, putting it into perspective.

- make sense of what we are feeling.

- know what to do with our feelings.

- problem-solve (often solutions to our difficulties arise as we talk about the situation with someone who cares)

SIX STEPS TO LISTENING TO YOUR SPOUSE'S FEELINGS AND PERSPECTIVE

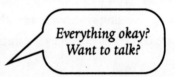

Everything okay?
Want to talk?

1. Be Emotionally Present.

It is very difficult to talk and share your heart with someone you feel is not there for you and really doesn't care. When you turn your shoulders toward your spouse, look into her eyes, and show you are interested, you not only help her make sense of and deal with her emotions but also draw the two of you closer.

Learn to listen with your full attention. It feels much safer and warmer when you tell your worries to someone who really cares. Listening will not only help your spouse make sense of what she is feeling, it will help her know what to do with the situation and draw the two of you closer together. How do you listen with your full attention?

- Turn your body toward your spouse.

- Keep eye contact.

- Show with your facial expressions and words that you care and are following along.

2. Name What Your Spouse Is Feeling.

> *Sounds like you had a rough day and were really hurt by your boss.*

When your spouse begins to share his experience and feelings, get on board for the "tour." As he talks, try to understand what he is saying and feeling. What situation is he describing? What is he feeling? What dragon is being raised, if any? Tell him what you hear him saying and what you sense he is feeling.

Don't dismiss, deny, or criticize your spouse's emotional experience. Instead, acknowledge it. There is something powerful about having our inner world seen and understood. When we hear someone name our inner emotional experience, it is very comforting and soothing. We feel "felt," and our experience is validated. When you name how your spouse might be feeling, your spouse will walk away thinking, *You are there for me, and you get me.*

A List of Feelings

Happy: hopeful, grateful, enthusiastic, optimistic, content, warm, close, connected, supported

Sad: disappointed, hurt, miserable, unappreciated, empty, lonely, abandoned, ignored, belittled

Angry: annoyed, disgusted, betrayed, mad, violated, unnoticed, pressured, cornered

Afraid: anxious, overwhelmed, tense, panicked, intimidated, pressured, insecure, uncertain

Surprised: shocked, stunned, taken aback, flabbergasted, astonished, startled, bowled over

---

Remember to look past the prickly porcupine quills or the cold icy walls of his anger and frustration to understand the emotional experience of his heart. Is he feeling hurt, disappointed, sad, fearful, alone, shamed, embarrassed, or betrayed?

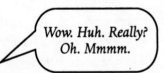

What did your boss say then?

3. Ask Questions to Understand your spouse's situation and experience— to invite your spouse to keep sharing.

Questions that show you care invite your spouse to keep sharing about her experience and emotions:

- "What happened after you got back from lunch? Was your boss waiting for you?"

- "You must have been surprised. What did you feel when your boss said that?"

Be sensitive, though, so that your questions don't appear as though you are probing for your own curiosity and gain. This line of questions can feel intrusive.

Wow. Huh. Really? Oh. Mmmm.

4. Listen and Follow with a Word

Words along with facial expressions say, "I am listening and following what you are saying and I am interested."

The most powerful way you can make your spouse feel heard and understood is often expressed with a simple word. Simple words, paired with a compassionate and interested attitude, are powerful signals to your spouse that you really care and are encouraging him to share his feelings and thoughts. Instead of problem solving, advice giving, and scolding, acknowledge what your spouse is saying with a word.

"Oh . . . hmm, I see. Wow! Really? Oh, my!" are simple words that say, "I care, I am listening, and I want you to keep talking."

> *Your boss is so critical.*
> *Sounds like you're tired*
> *of the battle.*

5. Express Understanding

Summarize the situation, acknowledge the emotion your spouse is feeling, and express your concern.

When you summarize what you think your spouse has been saying and name the emotion your spouse is feeling, along with your concern, you are expressing understanding.

- "Jessica is now walking, and it is so frustrating running after her. I can see why you're exhausted at the end of the day."

- "I know, the washing machine is barely a year old. It is so frustrating to have it overflow, adding to your already full schedule. I am so sorry it happened right before you had to leave to work. What a day!"

- "Oh my goodness, the day you choose to work from home and the Internet is down. I know, it does seem so unfair."

> *Mmmm. Yeah. I know this is*
> *so difficult for you. How can I*
> *support you in this? I'm here.*

6. Offer Comfort and Practical
Help that's Specific to Your Spouse's Situation and Feelings

Let your spouse know you care about his experience and feelings. The definition of *comfort* is a caring and soothing response that relaxes, consoles, reassures, calms, and eases the pain. Reach out and comfort your spouse in a way that is meaningful for him. Maybe touch your husband's arm, rub your hand across his back, touch your wife's face, or draw her in and, as you sigh, tell her everything will be okay.

Ask your spouse what he or she would feel is a meaningful, comforting response and remember it for times such as these. If you have told your spouse what is meaningful for you, and she forgets, remind her in the moment. Say, "It would feel good if you held me right now." Or "I wouldn't mind your rubbing my back."

Don't start a fight saying, "If you really cared about me you'd remember what is meaningful to me during times like this," or "If I have to tell you what is meaningful to me, then it won't come from your heart and you won't mean it," or "I don't want you to do something just because I tell you to." Scolding will not help your spouse remember what is meaningful to you. Instead, help your spouse succeed in comforting you. Both of you win: your spouse feels good about doing something that comforts you, and you feel the warmth of being comforted.

Then, find out what else your spouse needs regarding this situation. Maybe she would like your advice at this point, or maybe he wants you to be part of the solution. Perhaps she needs a night off, help with the house, a prayer, a date, an act of kindness, or a comforting word during this difficult time.

"During this difficult season, it would be nice if you asked me every day, 'How are you feeling?'"

"Can you please watch the kids so I can go see my mother and evaluate what I should do since her recent stroke?"

"Maybe I could take an evening class so I don't feel so trapped between work and house chores."

"Do you think you can help me organize the closet so I don't feel so scattered?"

QUESTIONS AND EXERCISES

1. Go back to your last argument and ask your spouse what he or she was trying to get you to understand.

   a. What was your spouse feeling besides angry, shut down, or frustrated?

   b. What makes it difficult for you to listen to and empathize with your spouse's perspective?

   c. Ask your spouse what would help to make him/her feel heard and understood during an argument.

2. Review the six steps of listening and identify the areas where you are strong and where you need to grow in terms of listening and empathizing.

3. What point of action can you take to improve listening and empathizing with your spouse?

NINE PRINCIPLE FOUR: COMPLAIN CONSTRUCTIVELY

IT IS AN ART TO SHARE A COMPLAINT SO YOUR POINT IS heard, understood, and considered. It is also an art to know how to receive a complaint—to be told you are wrong or hurtful.

Imagine this with me: You have a legitimate complaint, a genuine concern, an honest-to-goodness hurt you would like your spouse to understand. But your relationship system has given the signal that your spouse is not your safe haven, and your emotional brain has you ready to fight or flee. You feel yourself getting hot, angry, and very justified in reacting the way you do. But your complaint, concern, hurt, and explanation is lost in the *way* you say it. The argument boomerangs and becomes about how you reacted. What you wanted your spouse to understand is drowned out by the way you shared it. We have all found ourselves in this frustrating predicament, longing to know how we can complain so our spouse will listen and understand.

HOW YOU SAY IT

Keegan and Catrina know exactly what this is like.

> Keegan (on the phone): "I look forward to seeing you and Dad on the holidays as well."

Catrina (with an I-can't-believe-what-you-just-said tone of voice): "You'd better not have told your folks they can stay here over the holidays. I told you I wanted to talk with you and see if they can stay at a hotel. You let your mother walk all over you. You are so weak."

Keegan (disgusted and hurt): "Weak? I am weak? I can't believe you said that. I'm not staying here and listening to you put me down like that."

Catrina: "What? Now it becomes about me! You were the one who kept procrastinating and not wanting to discuss the options for your folks' visit. Now you get mad at me? Unbelievable!"

As you already know from past experience (and the previous chapters), a harsh start-up that expresses criticism and contempt does not make your spouse realize, "Oh my goodness, I see the wrong I have done. I am so sorry; let me do it differently." Rather, he is put on the defensive and protects his innocence with blame and criticism. When you start a conversation with anger, blame, and criticism, your spouse focuses on your hot negative emotion or accusation and is unable to hear your request, hurt, or heart. You are both left frustrated and feeling misunderstood.

So how can you communicate your complaint to your spouse, as well as how you feel when you are hurt, upset, and angry? How can you share your legitimate complaint in a way that your spouse can hear you?

In this chapter, I review several ideas that can make a difference in your ability to be heard. Try them. Talk through them with your spouse and find a way that draws the two of you together rather than pushes you apart.

STATE YOUR REQUEST UNDER THE ACACIA TREE

Begin by being clear about what you want, need, or expect. You can't complain about something you haven't talked about or for which you haven't established "protocols"—a set pattern or rule. If you and your spouse don't have a discussion outlining expectations regarding who will do what chores around the house, you can't get mad and blame each other when things don't get done.

Have what I call an *acacia-tree conversation*. In your safe place you share your perspectives, options, and ideas and establish clear expectations and guidelines. What is the protocol for getting the kids to bed? Who gets to spend what monies? What's okay regarding friends stopping by? How soon is "I will take out the trash in a minute"? Do we call each other if we will be ten minutes late? What about thirty minutes late? Will the first person home start dinner? What do we really want to happen tonight?

For example, you have been excited about going with your husband to a concert for your anniversary. You have a clear picture of how you hope the evening will turn out. Don't make your spouse read your mind, thinking, *If he really cares about me, he'll know I want to go to dinner before the concert, so he'll leave work early.* Crazy-making expectations will be a fast-track ticket to your feeling frustrated and disappointed.

Make your requests known up front, being clear and specific. To elicit the involvement of your spouse and make what you are asking a collaborative effort, ask for input. Allow him to tell you his perspective, need, and expectation about the issue.

If your spouse is making the request, make it of importance to you, but be honest about what *you* think, need, or are expecting. If you can't or don't want to comply, state so in a non-attacking manner. Putting off planning and discussing will only make matters worse. Don't say, "Yes, sure," knowing that you really don't want to or can't comply with the request.

Also, don't be quick to dismiss the idea without first exploring options. If your spouse says, "I would like to take a couple of hours every weekend to clean out the garage; let's start this Saturday," don't deflect:

Deflecting the request: "No, it won't work on Saturday. You cram too much stuff into our weekends."

Instead, consider your spouse's perspective:

Considering the request: "I wanted to play golf on Saturday, but let's see how we can fit everything into this weekend. Want to sit down and plan it out now or after dinner?"

HOW TO COMPLAIN SO YOU ARE HEARD

First, pick your complaints wisely. Often what we complain to our spouse about is related to personality and life differences. You might be efficient and get your chores done before you play. Your spouse might play first and, if there is time left, do his chores. Which way is right? To run a house smoothly, chores need to be done, but when and how fast is up for discussion. When you want your spouse to do it *your way*, be careful. You can request that your spouse pay the bills on time or do the dishes before going to bed. But can you really change your spouse so that now he or she values doing chores before playtime? Probably not.

Don't be too picky, fussy, bossy, controlling, or easily irritated. Pick your battles. Carefully choose your complaints. If you complain about everything, your spouse will . . . well, what do you think it would be like to live with someone who constantly complains?

But it is also not in the best interest of the marriage for you to put up with bad behavior or what you are uncomfortable with. As

Max said after a Haven of Safety Intensive, "I used to keep quiet about things. Why pick a battle? I can put up with a lot of things if I put my mind to it. But I realized I was not showing up for the relationship when I kept silent about my needs in an effort to duck and avoid conflict. I was shut down, and my wife could sense it."

For you to be connected with your spouse, to work toward being "one," you will each need to fold in your desires, hurts, and complaints. Now, let's look at six steps to complaining more effectively:

1. State Your Complaint

Describe to your spouse what you see as the problem, issue, or difference of opinion. State the problem in non-attacking terminology so your spouse can hear exactly what the problem is. Be specific rather than general.

Don't say, "You always make us late," or "You never consider me." Let your spouse know that you are not making broad-brush statements and implying that he or she is and always will be irresponsible, neglectful, unappreciated, or unvalued. Instead, complain about one particular action or area, affirming your spouse when you can. When you tell her you value her, but want to bring something to her attention, it makes her heart more willing to listen.

- "I appreciate all you do in the house, but can you make sure the kids pick up their toys from the driveway before I come home?"

- "I am really upset that you talked about your work through dinner and didn't even ask me how my meeting went. I felt unimportant to you."

2. Give Information

Rather than blame, put down, or attack your spouse's character, give your spouse information and facts. Explain the situation.

- "When you don't put a cover over the food in the refrigerator, the food is exposed to air and gets crusty."
- "When you don't tell me what checks you have written, I don't know what our balance is, and that sets us up for bounced checks."

It is less threatening when you describe the problem with information rather than describing your spouse as the problem. You can also state what you see are the consequences for what will happen if a particular task in question is not done.

- "If you don't mail out your mom's birthday present today, you will feel bad when you call her next week on her birthday and she expresses disappointment."
- "If you don't deposit the check today, the bills will not get paid, and we'll have late fees."

3. Share Your Feeling

You will probably have a strong feeling of hurt, disappointment, or frustration wrapped around your complaint. You feel frustrated that your spouse doesn't make up her mind. You feel angry when he misses an appointment. You feel alone and uncared for when he doesn't help with the dishes. You feel she is not a team member when she overspends an already established budget.

Share how you are feeling rather than attacking your spouse. And share your primary, softer feeling instead of your harsh, angry, and protective secondary feeling.

Don't attack: "Fine, don't invite me; see if I care. You are so insensitive."
Instead complain: "I feel very hurt and left out when you don't invite me to go with you."

4. Be Influenced—Weigh Your Spouse's Perspective

Listen to your spouse's perspective on the situation and weigh yours along with his. Allow what your spouse says and feels to impact your thoughts, emotions, and decisions. Does your spouse view this situation differently? Probably. Allow for that perspective. If you complain with only your view in front of you, your spouse will feel unseen, discounted, and misunderstood. Ask questions as you attempt to understand the situation from your spouse's perspective.

- "You got home later than I expected—what happened?"
- "I thought we weren't going to buy anything until you got your raise, but I see you bought a new camera. Help me understand what happened."

5. Review Solutions

Team together to find solutions to the situation. Remember your acacia-tree promise: You are husband and wife, you love each other, and of course, you want the best for each other. Explore options together and come up with suggestions to deal with the situation. Within the comfort of your safe-haven relationship and with the information you gave earlier, your spouse has the emotional space to team with you, think things through, and problem-solve.

- "I really don't want to be late, and you are still not dressed. What do you suggest?"
- "If you can't fix the toilet before the weekend, what do think about my calling in a plumber to make the repairs?"
- "What do you think would help us get the bills paid on time? Our life is so busy, maybe we can look into automatic payments through our bank."

6. Offer Brief Reminders

Keep your spouse on task with simple reminders. Be calm, share how you feel, and give information, letting your spouse know that you appreciate his efforts. By letting him see how important the task is to you and encouraging him, you will help him remember and succeed.

Reminding with an attack: "I am nervous you'll forget to pick up the cake on time. I usually can't count on you. Don't forget, or else . . ."

Reminding with appreciation: "Thanks for picking up the cake before three o'clock today. This party means a lot to me, and I really appreciate your help. Let me know if you can't do it." Or "You probably already know, but the post office closes in an hour. Thanks for your help with getting my mom's gift mailed."

FOR THE LISTENER

Often the shoe is on the other foot, and your spouse has a complaint against you. It takes equal skill to know how to hear and respond to those complaints.

1. Listen to the Complaint (it might be inside the criticism)

Although we dislike it when our spouse refutes or deflects our complaints, we often do the same to our spouse. If you defend instead of listen, your spouse won't feel heard and will feel as though you are the enemy, which leads him to fight harder to be heard. But when you listen, he'll feel safe and, in return, be able to listen to your perspective. Learn how to listen so each of you can feel heard.

- *Slow down.* Don't allow your spouse's complaint to raise your dragons. Pause. Take a breath. Let your heart rate stay normal.

- *Ask yourself, What is my spouse's complaint?* Before defending yourself or batting the complaint away, review the complaint. What is your spouse trying to get you to understand? Listen nondefensively:

  > *Oh, yes. He would like the toys picked up off the driveway when he comes home. He has requested that before. But he sure did wrap that legitimate complaint in a burrito of contempt. I wonder how I can let him know I understand his complaint while also letting him know how his critical comments hurt?*

- *Don't criticize your spouse's choice of words.* If the complaint is wrapped in criticism, blame, or rudeness, don't start an argument about how rude your spouse is. Yet, don't allow negativity to become the standard way of communicating with each other. Instead, listen to the complaint while letting the other know that bad manners are unnecessary.

John Gottman's research shows that the escalation of negativity by husbands and harsh start-ups and criticism by wives usually predict divorce. Although wives are well known for being critical and negative, research shows that when a wife adapts to and accepts her husband's negativity, the marriage is not enhanced or enriched, even though the wife would avoid conflict for the moment. I am not advocating that husbands and wives become critical watchdogs for each other's bad attitudes, but reminding you that when negativity creeps into a marriage and becomes the new normal, trouble only follows.

It is of great value to separate your spouse's legitimate complaint from the negative criticism. Let him or her know you heard the complaint, but also share how the critical comment hurt.

Kinder ways to say, "I can't hear you when you scream" are:

- "Slow down, sweetheart (*a soft start-up*). You don't need to yell and cuss at me to get me to listen (*giving information rather than attacking*). I know how frustrating it is to drive over a toy (*restating his legitimate complaint*), and I am more than willing to find a solution, but it's hard to do that when you're yelling at me."

- "Hey, I'm feeling attacked. Can you please rephrase your complaint in a kinder way?"

- "I think you have something legitimate to say, but all I hear is your angry yelling. Can you please say it another way?"

2. Be Willing to Self-Reflect

What truth is there in your spouse's complaint? Even though you may not see the situation the same way she does, is there some truth to what she is saying? Have you indeed been critical, defensive, procrastinating, harsh, or negative? Take a look at yourself. Yes, you have incredible strengths, but what about your weaknesses? Are they involved in this situation?

Your argument will only escalate, and neither of you will hear each other's point if you keep a defensive stance and an attitude of:

- *I disagree with what my wife is saying. I haven't done anything wrong; how can she be upset at me?*

- *If only my husband saw it my way, he wouldn't be hurt. So I'll keep stating my view in different ways.*

To be heard, you have to listen, and part of listening is to admit it when your spouse is pointing straight to your weaknesses.

3. Don't React as Though Attacked

If your spouse is trying to state a legitimate complaint, slow down. Don't be quick to defend yourself or explain why you did what you did. Don't be dismissive, even though you may not agree with the complaint. Try to understand his perspective. Why is he upset? What is he trying to get you to understand? Why is this important to him? If you ignore your spouse, brush him off, and say, "I don't want to talk about it now," or "That's not true," or "Well, I have things I am disappointed about as well," you teach your spouse that the only way to get through to you is to turn the complaints up a few notches, get harsher, and criticize. Then the hurts begin to build.

4. Express Understanding

Let your spouse know you understand the complaint:

- "You've had a long day at work and you would really like the kids to clear their toys off the driveway before you come home. I can understand that. I know how upsetting that is to you."

Expressing understanding for your spouse's complaint is not always easy to do, especially if you feel the complaint is not warranted. However, when complaints are not heard and responded to, resentment and hurt build a wall between the two of you.

Reflect back to your spouse what you think the legitimate complaint is. Show that you care about his perspective and feelings even though you might not agree with them. Let your spouse know that you have heard his complaint, will take it seriously, self-reflect, and respond in a considerate manner.

- "Your complaint is that I don't help around the house unless I am asked several times. Well, I will need to think about that. Off the top of my head, I feel I do lots of things, but I want to consider what you are saying. I will think about when those times were because I would like to change that."

5. Share Your Perspective and Find Solutions Together

"I just want you to understand me like you want me to understand you" is at the core of each argument. Remember that. Aim to work out a win-win for both of you. Be part of the solution rather than fuel for the argument.

- *Share your perspective.*

  Fold your view and perspective into the conversation. Do this in a way that does not dismiss or discount your spouse's complaint.

    - "I know you are mad at me. I can understand how disappointed you were when you walked in and saw the ants still on the countertop. But I would like for you to understand that I intended to clean it up. I just think our expectations for *when* were different."
    - "I can see why you felt left out and hurt last night. But I finally said, 'I am going to the movies on my own' because I had asked you all afternoon if you would go with me, and you said no."

- *Find solutions together.*

  Zachary confesses to Ava, "I forgot to mail the bill today. I know you are very mad and frustrated, but are there any other options? Can I pay the bill over the phone?"

Refraining from telling him how she hates the mad rush and pressure he puts on her when he procrastinates, Ava begins to problem-solve with Zachary. Neither does she start talking about how he should be more responsible. Instead, she teams with him to think of options: "Well, I think it is too late for that. But doesn't the mail at the main post office in Pasadena leave at 8:30 instead of the regular 6:00 around town?"

Zachary doesn't make excuses but says, "Great, if you'll watch the kids, I will quickly drive over there. I'm sorry for the confusion I create when I procrastinate. I know you kept reminding me to mail the bill. I'll be back. Bye."

6. Find Ways to Turn Toward Your Spouse and Repair Your Connection

Making attempts to resolve the disagreement and repair hurt hearts is of great value in helping you and your spouse stay emotionally connected. When you know your spouse is hurt by what you said, did, or didn't say or do, find ways to repair the rupture, to reconnect.

Express tenderness. Use humor to clear the air (but not to avoid talking about complaints). Bring up a neutral topic, such as, "Hey, I saw that Gus's Guitar Shop is having a sale." Slowly melt and turn toward each other.

Remember, what you do when you are not arguing is just as important as how you argue.

QUESTIONS AND EXERCISES

1. What unresolved arguments or issues would you like to discuss with your spouse under the safety of your acacia tree? Write out each of your issues, concerns, or complaints in a considerate, nonblaming manner.

2. What information will help your spouse understand why this complaint, concern, or request is important to you?

3. List the feelings such as hurt, frustration, and disappointment you want your spouse to understand regarding this concern.

4. What truth is there in your spouse's perspective regarding your concern?

5. What dragon could your complaint trigger in your spouse? How can you be sensitive to that?

6. What truth is there in your spouse's perspective regarding your complaint?

7. With your spouse, explore solutions to your complaint or concerns, remembering to soften your statements in order to avoid triggering each other's defensiveness.

8. Tell your spouse how you appreciate his or her listening to and considering your concerns.

TEN PRINCIPLE FIVE: MAKE AMENDS

HOW A COUPLE ARGUES CAN DEEPLY WOUND A HUSBAND AND wife's heart. The inability to apologize, forgive, and heal the wounding done is what tears them apart. Because arguments hurt, apologizing and forgiving is of vital importance. If your hurts are not resolved, they accumulate and cause you to emotionally disconnect and protect yourselves in defensive ways. Since you and your spouse probably hurt each other in one way or another every day of your lives, you need to learn how to resolve those hurts on an ongoing basis.

> Do not be bitter or angry or mad. Never shout angrily or say things to hurt others. Never do anything evil. Be kind and loving to each other, and forgive each other just as God forgave you in Christ.
>
> —Ephesians 4:31–32 (NCV)

Your ability to repair your arguments determines whether or not your hearts remain hurt and disconnected or healed and reconnected. The key to not allowing your arguments to destroy your relationship is knowing how to apologize, forgive, turn toward each other, and reconnect as soon after your argument as possible.

Before looking at a process for repairing your relationship after arguments, I want to encourage you to stay vulnerable and open with your spouse despite the potential of hurt between the two of you. After you have apologized and forgiven each other, it is important to know how to turn toward each other and emotionally reconnect. It is a risk, but protecting yourself from ever being hurt again by your spouse's words or actions is not possible. You can't live behind a wall to ward off the hurtful arrows. The fact is, you will be hurt again. (I am not talking about marital betrayals, but rather everyday arguments that hurt.) Your spouse will say things, forget to do things, and hurt your feelings. Unless you take the chance to trust and come close again, you won't be able to truly heal and emotionally reconnect. So remember, after forgiving, risk coming close again.

Research shows that what impacts your marriage is not that you argue over your differences, but rather how you argue and whether or not you are able to repair your hurts after you argue. As you have learned in earlier chapters, if you argue using criticism, contempt, blame, and withdrawing, you will hurt each other and disconnect. But if you are *unable* to reconnect in a way that is meaningful, then your marriage will move toward an empty relationship that revolves around duty, chores, and separate lives.

The point is: don't ruminate, hold resentment, or spend your days sulking. Life is too short. You both deserve a meaningful life filled with a bit of happiness. And life is difficult as it is. You both need a friend, a lover, someone who can be there for you and support you. So don't spend more time arguing than you absolutely need. Resolve your conflicts well so you can return to the shelter and safety of your acacia tree and enjoy each other as soon as possible.

I want to assure you that I understand how very difficult it is to apologize, forgive, and reconnect if trust has been betrayed in the marriage. I have sat in the counseling room with many couples facing such struggles. I have seen how affairs, pornography, workaholism, alcoholism, gambling, and other addictions tear down the marriage bond. These kinds of hurts require a bit more time and focus—a special kind of process for lasting healing to occur. I recommend counseling from a qualified pastor or marriage counselor to walk alongside you on this journey. I have worked with many couples, and I am able to say with certainty and confidence: have hope—healing is possible and doable.

Whether you catch your spouse leaving the toilet seat up again or using the last check without replacing it or scratching the car or forgetting your anniversary, all marital hurts require you to apologize, forgive, and reconnect. I will show here two different scenarios. The first process outlines how to apologize, forgive, and reconnect when smaller misunderstandings happen, such as when you feel your spouse took what you said the wrong way. The second is how to apologize, forgive, and reconnect after deep emotional hurts. Even though these processes are similar, I offer them as examples of how to share your hearts and work toward healing. There are no exact steps for this; you and your spouse will need to finetune a process that works for you.

> When you are angry, do not sin, and be sure to stop being angry before the end of the day.
>
> —Ephesians 4:26 (NCV)

THE ART OF APOLOGIZING AND FORGIVING

"I didn't mean it that way. Why do I still have to apologize?"

"I felt hurt by what you said."

"I did not say what you said I did, and I did not mean it the way you took it."

"But I still feel hurt. Why can't you just apologize for hurting me?"

"I didn't mean it that way; why should I apologize?"

Just about every couple who enters my counseling doors asks this question: "Dr. Morris May, isn't there a reality, a factual truth of what we actually did or didn't say in an argument?"

Even though there are certain factual realities, such as the fact that both you and your spouse walked into the room, how you make sense of what happened, or how each of you perceive what happened, is influenced by the lens through which you viewed the event. Your beliefs, personality, quirks, dragons, and preferences will all shape how you view a particular situation.

So when your wife walked into the kitchen, you made a judgment about *how* she walked in. She could say that she "quickly walked in and out." You might say that she "rudely stomped in and out." She could refute that and say that her "heart intention" was not to be rude. But somehow you interpreted her body language and mannerisms as being rude.

Now what is the reality? Did she really walk in "briskly" or "rudely"? For each of you, your reality is real. It is not of value to find the "real reality" and confirm who is right or wrong, but rather to accept each other's interpretation and go on from there.

Don't try to find the reality or truth of what happened.

Fighting about who-said-what will only trigger an I-did-not-say-it-that-way . . . yes-you-did argument. A go-nowhere, pointless argument.

Instead, work toward acknowledging each other's perspective and the emotions each of you felt. Then work toward comforting each other. This is a powerful way to heal hurts that find a way of accumulating and weighing down your relationship.

Understand, Acknowledge, and Comfort Each Other's Perspective

This scenario might sound typical of your arguments where you each disagree on what was said and how it was intended to come across:

Jerry left for work early one morning. Isabel did not hear him say good-bye but only heard what sounded to her like the door slamming behind him. Jerry says that he said good-bye, but because Isabel was in a bad mood, she did not hear him, and he did not slam the front door.

1. Gain understanding of each other's perspective.

Discover and recognize each other's view of what happened. Remember, you will probably have different views of the situation. Accept the fact: you and your spouse have different perspectives. There is no right or wrong view, just each of your own views. Even though you disagree on what happened, come to a neutral ground. Give your spouse's perspective the same weight as you give yours.

Jerry's view: "Isabel was in her *quiet* mood when I left. I shouted good-bye and closed the front door."

Isabel's view: "Jerry was still hurt from the argument the night before and left without saying good-bye, but he slammed the front door."

2. Acknowledge each other's feelings: you were hurt, and I didn't say it that way.

Accept the fact that your spouse felt hurt by what you did or said, regardless of what you feel you intended to do or say. Even if you feel you did not make your statement in a hurtful manner, she feels you did. Your arguing with her to get her to feel differently won't work. It will only keep her in a defensive position, protecting herself and attempting to convince you of her feelings.

Listen to Jerry and Isabel's attempt to get to the truth about what happened so each person's feelings can be acknowledged and comforted. They aren't able to find the "reality" and get stuck:

> Isabel: "It hurt when you left without saying good-bye
> and slammed the door."

Jerry: "I did not slam the door, and I yelled, 'Bye.' You
just didn't hear me."

Isabel: "You didn't say good-bye, and I definitely heard
the door slam."

When you and your spouse get stuck in a similar argument like
Jerry and Isabel, you could keep arguing about whether or not the
door was slammed or good-bye was said. You could end the conversation by concluding one of three things:

- *You are wrong.*

  You can conclude that your spouse is clearly wrong
  and that with some persuasion he or she will see it. You
  are certain you are right.

  Jerry: "I did not slam the door and I said good-bye. You
  are being ridiculous and just trying to pick a fight."

  Isabel: "I am not stupid; I know what a door slamming
  sounds like. You just can't admit to being rude."

- *We agree to disagree.*

  This is the "I give up" stage where you both quit the
  fight and conclude that you're right, and your spouse just
  can't see it. But there is nothing you can do about it.

  Isabel: "Fine, whatever. But I know what I heard."

  Jerry: "Well, I know what I did."

Although it stops the argument from going anywhere,
this position does not foster resolve or closure. Neither
of you feels heard or accepted. In our scenario, Isabel
does not feel her hurt has been validated or comforted,
and Jerry feels wrongly accused and misunderstood. These

strong emotions are tucked away and come out in their next argument.

- *We understand how each of us could feel the way we do.*

  You can turn toward each other by looking at the situation through each other's lens, trying to understand why you each feel the way you do, and then expressing understanding and comfort. This is of utmost importance, and here is how it looks in detail.

3. Offer comfort for each other's view.

Jerry: "I thought you were being rude and argumentative."

Isabel: "I thought you were being controlling and not willing to hear my view."

Jerry: "If you thought I was not willing to listen to you, I can see how hurt you must have felt."

Isabel: "Yeah, I did not get the impression that you were open to a discussion. But if you were open to a discussion, then my accusing you of being a steamroller must have been hurtful to you."

In this scenario, what each spouse was saying to each other was in essence the following:

"If you saw the situation this way _____, then it makes sense that you feel this way _____."

Even if you disagree about the legitimacy of the lens through which your spouse views a situation, it is best to come to an understanding that if your spouse saw the situation the way he did, then it makes sense that he felt the way he did.

Remember, your spouse views situations through the lens of his or her vulnerabilities, fears, and dragons. What she has seen before she will see again. If he was raised in a critical home, he will probably be sensitive to criticism (or easily able to be critical because that way of seeing things is familiar). So whether or not you feel he shouldn't be sensitive to criticism, he is. Further, the way you react when your spouse feels criticized can either confirm his or her dragon (the world is critical) or refute the dragon (I thought the world was critical, but look, my spouse is accepting).

It is always in the best interest of your relationship to be accepting and understanding—always looking at the situation from each other's perspective, then responding with *both* perspectives in mind.

- *Responding with comfort*

  Isabel: "I was hurt. Not only did I think you left without saying good-bye, but when I heard the door slam, I was certain you were mad at me."

  Jerry: "I can see how hurt and sad you'd feel if you thought I didn't say good-bye and slammed the door as a way of letting you know I was mad at you. Come here; let me give you a hug. I don't want you to feel that. When I left, my intention was not to hurt you."

  Isabel: "Thanks, I appreciate that. And if you really didn't intend to leave for work in an angry manner, then you must feel very frustrated when I keep insisting that you did. I am sorry I got so upset at you."

  Jerry: "I appreciate that."

4. Express what you need.

After you acknowledge and accept each other's perspective and comfort each other's feelings, express what you need and ask your spouse what he or she needs.

Isabel: "But can I ask you to come and say good-bye to me when you leave for work? It means a lot to me."

Jerry: "Sure. But can I ask you not to say such hurtful things when you are upset at me?"

Isabel: "Yeah, I don't mean half the things I say when I am so hurt by you. I get so angry when I feel you won't consider my view. I have been watching what I say, but I will keep working on that."

Jerry: "Thanks. I will also try not to be so defensive when you bring up something I have done wrong."

5. Turn toward each other and reconnect.

Although I have intentionally not told many stories of my husband, Mike, and me (I share all our fun and meaningful stories in my Haven of Safety Conferences), I include this incident. Let me summarize a conversation we had recently regarding men apologizing.

"It is hard for a man to turn toward his wife and apologize when he feels he hasn't done anything wrong," Mike explained.

"So why do men eventually apologize?" I asked.

"Maybe because we realize that fighting to be right actually destroys what we value the most. We are actually wanting to be heard and respected by our wives. And when a husband fights to be right rather than tries to understand his wife, he pushes his wife away. It is not worth it in the end. We not only don't get to be right, but we are also disconnected from our wife. Who wins?"

"So should husbands just give in?"

"No, giving in only builds a wall around a man's heart. Sometimes it is important for a husband to share his perspective. But there comes a point where a husband has to let go of the battle and understand his wife. Apologize, forgive, and love her. That is in the best interest of one's marriage. Sometimes it is best to do this sooner than later."

As Mike spoke I realized that this truth also applied to wives. As women, we can sometimes get angry quickly, brew and stew long and hard, and be very articulate as we do it. We often feel we have the "right to say something" with the wrong manner at the wrong time. We need to admit to it sooner and find a way of communicating differently. There also comes a point when a wife has to "give up the battle," apologize for her part, and forgive. What good is it to fight to the bitter end, punish your husband, and end up bitter, resentful, and disconnected? It is true: forgiveness covers much hurt and wrongs.

APOLOGIZING, FORGIVING, AND HEALING THE HURTS OF YOUR HEART

Sometimes when you remind your spouse of the many times he or she has let you down or hurt you, the response you hear is "Not this again" or "Haven't we talked about that enough?" or "Why do you keep bringing that up?" and "I will never hear the end of it. I will forever be punished for what happened."

How do the hurts and wounds that keep you and your spouse disconnected get healed and resolved? Here is a process that has been useful to many couples in my intensives.

1. Affirm your safe haven.

Frankly, most of your hurts are because you felt your spouse was not your safe haven, so to begin the process of making amends and healing, reaffirm your safe place. Let your spouse know that even though you are upset, you care about her very much and want to find a way of resolving your hurt so you can reconnect.

"You know I appreciate how hard you work for the family, but I am so disappointed that you came home late. You promised me you would be home at five o'clock. I would like to finish the evening connected, but I need you to understand why I am so hurt."

2. Tell your spouse you are hurt.

Be gentle and use manners as you tell your spouse what hurts. If you scold, criticize, or use anger to express your hurt, remember, it will not switch your spouse's lightbulb on, causing an ah-ha moment about your hurt. Rather, it will only trigger in your spouse a protective and defensive attitude against you. To be heard, be gentle, be considerate, and use manners.

Then tell your spouse what you are disappointed about. Remember the chapter on the relationship system? It is because he means so much to you that you feel hurt, angry, and disappointed when he is not close and there for you. Your relationship alarm sounds off because he is so important to you, and when that happens, your initial reaction is an angry protest. You are protesting his broken promise or his being gone because he means so much to you. Don't forget to say this when you express your hurt and disappointment.

Most times the first emotion you will feel when hurt by your spouse is anger. Don't only express your thorny, angry, protesting emotions saying, "Why are you late? You lied to me. How can I trust you? How many times do we have to go over this? I need your help on the nights I have my class."

Remember to add your heartfelt experience, softer hurts, and needs, such as "When you are late I am left alone carrying the burden of the kids and home. I need to know you are my partner and that you will make me a priority. I am very hurt."

If you started your encounter with your spouse in a harsh manner (maybe added a few criticisms), you probably need to apologize for the way you reacted before your spouse can truly hold your hurt. Ask for the chance to start over.

A simple, "I am sorry I came on so harshly when you walked in the door . . . but I was so counting on your helping me with the kids tonight. I am sorry for hurting you with my anger. If I can start over in a more gentle way, I would really like for you to understand why I am hurt."

3. Listen to your spouse's perspective.

After you have expressed why you are hurt and disappointed, give your spouse a chance to explain herself. Listen to her perspective. Try to understand why it made sense for her to do what she did. Why was she late? Why did he not lock the door? Why did he forget to take the package to the post office? Even if it sounds like he is making excuses, just listen. Try to understand what the situation looked like from her perspective. When she feels heard, she will be more willing to listen and hear you.

Consider Kurt and Anne's story. It's a powerful one. Shortly after Anne's mother died, her father was in a serious car accident. Anne asked her husband, Kurt, to fly with her to visit her father. He said he had to wait a few days to finish up some work but for her to go on ahead. While on the airplane Anne broke down crying.

Anne: "I was deeply hurt and felt abandoned by Kurt."

Kurt: "I am so tired of hearing this story. She will never let it go."

Dr. Morris May: "What happened, Kurt? Why did you not go with Anne?"

Kurt: "I don't know. Something inside of me froze that week. I lost my parents at a very early age. Anne's mother had just died, and it was very hard on me. I didn't want to face death again. I felt so bad for Anne, and I didn't know how to comfort her."

Anne: "I didn't know this was what you were feeling."

Dr. Morris May: "Does his experience make a difference to your hurt?"

Anne: "Yes, of course. I thought he was heartless and didn't
care about me. Now I know he actually cared . . . but
was scared. If I had known, we could have comforted
each other."

4. Apologize.

The sentences you use when you apologize are really very simple,
but you'll need a large heart with a desire to love deeply. When apologizing, be specific. Mention the event. Also include the hurt your
spouse felt. Be genuine.

"I am sorry I came home late and added extra pressure to
your day."

"I am sorry I didn't consider you when I made plans for this
weekend. It made you feel unimportant."

Try not to do it again. Find the bit of truth in what happened. What
is your spouse accusing you of doing? Self-reflect. Is it something in
which you need to grow? Do you need to change?

Let me make this real:

You were late, yes? Yes. You tend to be late because you procrastinate and don't keep an eye on the clock, yes? Yes. And this happens
often, yes? Yes.

Then how can you grow and learn to be more aware of time and
not put things off until the last minute? True, your spouse needs to
learn to accept you and be gentle around your not-so-perfect edges.
But you need to admit to the areas in which you need to grow and
make growing in these areas important to you.

5. Forgive.

Forgiveness, according to my father, Dr. Archibald Hart, is defined
as "giving up my right to hurt you back." This is a worthy motto to

add to your acacia-tree promise: No matter what, we will give up our right to hurt each other back. We will work toward understanding, apologizing, and forgiving. This is for the good of our relationship.

Learn to forgive, preferably before the sun sets each day. Forgive because it is the best thing you can do for yourself and the marriage. Resentment, bitterness, and unforgiveness are powerful emotions that destroy you from the inside out. Forgive because God forgave you. If God forgives you, then you can't expect to hold unforgiveness in your heart toward your spouse. Besides, you want your spouse to forgive you, don't you? Oh, but you probably think that the things you do to your spouse are not half as bad as the things your spouse does to you, right? Then you need to practice forgiveness even more.

In the Bible, we are also repeatedly told of the amazing and healing power of love and forgiveness. "Most importantly, love each other deeply, because love will cause people to forgive each other for many sins" (1 Pet. 4:8 NCV).

"I am sorry I was late. I did not mean to ruin your evening. That was not my intention. I need to manage my time better."

"I know. I forgive you. Thanks for being willing to grow."

6. Tell your spouse what you need to be comforted.

Help your spouse win by telling him what you need to feel connected and comforted. You could say, "If my husband really loved and understood me, he would know what I need to be comforted." That is actually not true. Your spouse may care very much but just needs to be reminded. Remember, when your spouse's emotional brain senses danger (such as your anger, signaling that he is in trouble), it does not have access to the how-to-comfort-and-nurture parts of the brain. He actually needs help remembering. So instead of sulking because he needs to be reminded, help him give you what you long for: comfort. Tell him what you need in clear words. Maybe you need him to just listen and, through his body language, let you know that he cares about your hurt. Or maybe you need to hear your spouse say, "I understand why you are upset." Maybe you need a hug, a kiss, a gentle touch.

7. Be soothable.

It is sometimes difficult to allow the kind, comforting words of your spouse to melt your anger. Sometimes you want to be in a bad mood for a while—let off some steam, get the hurt off your chest. Although being upset feels justified, even satisfying in the moment, it is not productive. It is tough to then switch our attitude from negative and prickly to warm and connecting. For many people, this takes time. But it does not need to take a long time.

Allow you and your spouse to continue the day connected, to have a "happy ending" to your dinner or day. Allow yourself to absorb your spouse's love, help, and comfort. If you reject your spouse's olive branch or expression of care and comfort, you are only sabotaging yourself.

Think about it. Imagine that your husband (or wife) usually comes home from work at 5:00. On this particular night, he comes home at 6:15. What are you wanting from 5:00 to 6:00? Exactly—for your husband to come home and help! He now arrives home at 6:15. Yes, he is late again.

When he walks in the front door, you share your complaint (without criticism), and now he is aware of how upset you are. He feels bad about it and expresses it. But do you offer him a way of making amends and reconnecting? It is now 6:45, and you have sulked and slammed a pot or two for half an hour, occasionally telling him how tired you are and how busy you have been. Is your evening ruined? No. You actually have a chance to finish the evening warm and reconnected if you choose. You are not going to solve the why-can't-you-get-off-work-on-time? issue before you go to bed. That would be a problem-solving conversation you could have with each other later, when you both have the time. But for the remainder of the evening, your husband could be a comfort, resource, and help to you.

What purpose would be served by being unforgiving, resentful, or pushing your spouse away with sulking and anger? Will it get your husband to understand how hurt you are and how you need him to be on time? Probably not. He will more than likely walk away thinking, *Boy, she is upset. I'd better stay away from her tonight.* Instead, tell your spouse what you need him to understand about your hurt. Then tell him what practical help and comfort you might need. Forgive him. And if you are the one who was late, even though you were the recipient of a harsh start-up when you first walked in the door, allow yourself to soften and reconnect. Team together to finish the evening. Then when the chores are done, allow yourself to lie in your wife's arms and absorb her comfort. If you stay angry and disconnect, you will only push her away as well as not get what you need, which is to have your wife be a friend and helpmate, attentive, and close.

Here's how a more soothing conversation might sound:

"Your being late put a lot of pressure on me tonight. Thanks for doing the dishes. I appreciate the help. It's nice watching the movie with you right now. It's a nice way to end a busy day."

Or "I know the route you took turned out to be the long way around. Sorry I got upset with you. I was so looking forward to this evening. But we are here now, and the fresh sea air smells good. It's nice to get away and be together. I love you."

8. Plan for a safe haven, acacia-tree conversation.

Sometimes what you and your spouse need is a specific problem-solving conversation. More than likely, that conversation will not occur in the heat of an argument. You can't be logical, empathetic, or understanding when your emotional brains have hijacked your thinking brains. Instead, set time aside to sit under the shade and safety of your acacia tree and talk about the problem that needs addressing. In the calm of your acacia tree, you can put each of your opinions and perspectives on the table, think through options, and find solutions.

Maybe you do need a conversation about why your spouse is consistently late coming home from work. Maybe you need to change the "policy" regarding how weekend plans are made . . . or the policy on how often to call and check in with each other when away on business trips . . . or who checks to make sure the front door is locked at night.

"I was very hurt by your being home late tonight. Maybe this weekend we can talk and you can help me understand why it is so difficult for you to get away from the office on time. But now I would like to just sit here and enjoy a cup of coffee with you."

APOLOGIZE, FORGIVE, AND RECONNECT

You and your mate will possibly argue every day of your married life. The two most important things that impact your marriage are how you argue and how you turn toward each other and make amends after your arguments. The critical words that are said, the old offenses that are constantly brought up, the accusations of character, the refusal to empathize, and the inability to affirm the other person's perspective all can destroy the safe connection in your marriage. If you can't apologize, forgive, and then reconnect, you will not be resilient and able to bounce back from the ongoing bumps and bruises of arguing. Knowing how to apologize and forgive on a daily basis is key to avoiding the damage of your arguments.

Apologizing and forgiving becomes difficult in our what-about-my-needs? society. Our culture teaches us to apologize only when we need to and demand an apology from those who slight us. But God asks more from us. God talks about forgiveness being part of loving those around us. When we are hurt or when we have hurt another, God asks us to have mercy, kindness, humility, gentleness, and patience. This is required for a safe-haven marriage.

Read what Colossians 3:12–14 says about love and forgiveness:

"God has chosen you and made you his holy people. He loves you. So you should always clothe yourselves with mercy, kindness, humility, gentleness, and patience. Bear with each other, and forgive each other. If someone does wrong to you, forgive that person because the Lord forgave you. Even more than all this, clothe yourself in love. Love is what holds you all together in perfect unity" (NCV).

When does fighting to be right outweigh the good of your marriage? You can either push to be right, but hurt and alienate your spouse, or you can try hard to understand your spouse's perspective and, from that place of understanding, apologize, forgive, and reconnect. You do this not for your own happiness, but for the greater good of your marriage. We are called to love and care for each other, to be safe havens for each other, and in everything strive to build up, encourage, show understanding, have patience, and forgive.

QUESTIONS AND EXERCISES

1. As you were reading through this chapter, what hurt or offense came to mind that is a point of unforgiveness in your heart?

2. What was your spouse's perspective on the incident that hurt or offended you?

3. Recognize and acknowledge your part in the situation and tell your spouse. If need be, apologize to your spouse.

4. How have you continued to punish your spouse for what he or she did to hurt you? What Bible verse or prayer can you say to give you strength as you release your right to hurt your spouse back?

5. What do you and your spouse need in order to open up your hearts, trust, and reconnect with each other?

ELEVEN PRINCIPLE SIX: RECONNECT AND ENJOY EACH OTHER

IT TAKES A LOT OF ENERGY TO ARGUE. TRYING TO BE HEARD and understood can be stressful, leaving you hurt, tired, and drained. As you have discovered in this book, arguing puts you and your spouse in the fight-or-flight mode, pumping stress hormones throughout your body. After an argument, it is of vital importance to repair your relationship and allow the stress hormones to drop and your body systems return to a normal resting state. When the argument is over, your hurts have been repaired and once again you feel safe and connected to your spouse. But constant arguing can keep your body in a stressful state that, over time, can have a negative impact not only on your relationship but also on your health.

LET GOOD TIMES BOOKEND YOUR ARGUMENTS

This is why, when you and your spouse are *not* arguing, you need all of the positive, soothing, peaceful, comforting, and happy interactions you can possibly have. It is essential that emotionally connecting exchanges, meaningful interactions, and good times bookend your arguments.

When you are not arguing, turn toward each other and enjoy each other. Make the most of each interaction. Open your hearts toward each other, laugh, touch, play, share, and fill your minutes with pleasant times together. Make sure the positive times you have together outweigh the stress and struggle of your arguments. Make sure your minds and hearts are filled with good, positive experiences with each other. When you feel emotionally connected, you are able to trust your spouse's intentions and more easily bounce back from the negativity of your arguments. You are able to be fully present and fully connected.

What are the important positive interactions you and your spouse need to experience as bookends to your arguments? What will help you enjoy each other? Here are five important things to help you reconnect and renew positive interactions with your spouse.

1. Focus on Your Spouse's Positives

Don't let the negative thoughts and feelings about your spouse take over the positive ones. It is not productive to ruminate or go over and over all the negative traits of your spouse.

Whatever is good, think of that. The more you think of the negative things your spouse has done, the more negative your thoughts become, and the more certain you are of their truth. Instead, remind yourself of the good qualities of your husband and why you fell in love with him in the first place. Remember why you are so proud of your wife and what makes you look forward to coming home to her.

Whatever is noble and respectable about your spouse, think about that. Whatever is good and wonderful about your spouse, think about that. Begin to replace the "garbage" thoughts with honoring thoughts.

What needs to change, focus on it. This does not mean that you ignore what your spouse does that hurts you. Rather, find your constructive complaint and then fill in the rest with positive thoughts of your spouse's strengths. Keep your complaints contained. Don't general-ize or make large leaps from a specific I-don't-like-it-when-you-do-this to a broad you-never-do-anything-good. This will give you a negative mind-set and won't lead to anything productive. Instead, keep focused on the specific thing you want your spouse to under-stand or change.

Tell your spouse when you begin to protect your heart. If you are hurt and find yourself pulling away and protecting your heart, tell your spouse. Tell your wife that you don't want to stay unplugged from the relationship, but when she demeans you in an argument, her words really hurt. The mere act of sharing your hurt and that you are protecting your heart from being hurt will be in and of itself a connecting interaction.

Begin to talk about your resentment, hurt, and fear of being vulnerable rather than remaining in your negative thoughts. Take the steps necessary to forgive your spouse and to wash away all resentment. Let's be honest; can you truly have fun with your hus-band when you are busy protecting your heart from being hurt by him? Can you really feel connected to your wife when you are reviewing all the times she called you a jerk? Probably not.

2. Turn Toward Each Other

Safe-haven marriages are not built on dinner dates, flowers, gifts, or weekend getaways. Although those are wonderful surprises that add to an already emotionally connected marriage, they are not the foundation for a couple to feel safe, close, and emotionally con-nected. Instead, what keeps a couple's love alive is how they turn toward each other and connect in the everyday mundane moments of life. It is in the small moments of a day—simple moments—that add up to make their relationship a sweet, tender, and meaningful friendship.

The power of turning toward each other. Surprising things happen when a couple is consistently able to turn toward each other. When a husband and wife respond to each other's attempts to connect, the bond that ties them together is strengthened.

This is often seen in small interactions, such as when a husband and wife pass each other in the hallway, and the wife smiles and says, "Hey, handsome." Her husband winks. A flirtatious interaction keeps them feeling noticed by the other.

Or the greeting when a wife comes home from work and her husband says, "Hey, you're home. I just got back from the doctor myself," and she answers, "Yeah, traffic was bad. Oh yes, how was the doctor's appointment?" And a simple end-of-the-day conversation meanders along, connecting the two to their individual days.

Or the casual small talk when a couple is driving to church and the wife says, "Looks like they're painting the bank," and her husband responds, "Yeah, finally. But can you believe that color?" There is silence, and as he puts his hand on the center armrest, his wife reaches over and holds his hand. Click! Their hearts connect. Life feels warm.

These interchanges keep a couple turning toward each other, noticing each other, listening to each other, sensitive to each other, responding to each other, and when accumulated, *connected* to each other.

Turning down attempts to connect. When a partner attempts to connect in a small manner and it is not received or responded to, it has a negative impact on the marriage. John Gottman's research repeatedly shows that couples in unhappy marriages hardly ever turn toward each other and rarely make overtures for connecting.

Turning away from your spouse's attempt to connect is done in various ways. One way is when you give a passive response, acting as though you are preoccupied, and ignore the attempt to connect. "I saw Jack today" is answered with a disinterested, "Huh, oh, mmm."

Or you interrupt your spouse and change the subject: "I saw Jack today" is answered with a "What? Hand me that pen."

Or you show irritation for being bothered by such a silly comment or question: "What do you want now? Can't you see I have more important things to do? You are not starting that again, are you?"

If you respond this way, your spouse will feel embarrassed and shamed for risking to reach out and connect with you. When you repeatedly respond this way, your spouse will stop turning toward you. Why should she? Instead, she will keep to her side of the fence and after a while, will close her heart toward you. This is a dangerous place for you or your spouse to be in your marriage.

So the next time you ignore your wife after she says something that seems small and insignificant, pause and ask yourself, *Did I just turn down my wife's attempt to connect? Did I let go of an opportunity to explore my wife's world and miss a chance to connect?* Then make a 180-degree turn and go back and respond. It will lower your stress levels, increase your feel-good hormones, and keep the two of you connected.

Finding time to connect. Connecting with each other becomes difficult in the midst of the busy schedules most couples keep. The fast-paced lifestyle most couples live is hard on a marriage. Time becomes difficult to find, and time together without the stress, worries, or demands of life becomes almost impossible. Many couples have less than an hour a night and a few hours over the weekend to build their friendship and enjoy each other.

Most husbands and wives feel that their marriages can be put on autopilot and that everything will work out just fine, even without making an effort to build their friendship. If you and your spouse wait and do nothing, nothing will ever change. Don't let neglect kill the friendship in your marriage.

The Stress Response

You perceive danger with your spouse's negative comment. Your body triggers the stress response and gets you ready to react.

Stress Response

- Hypothalamic-pituitary-adrenal system (HPA) is activated.
- Steroid hormones are released (glucocorticoids), including cortisol (the primary stress hormone).
- Neurotransmitters are released (catecholamines), including dopamine, norepinephrine, and epinephrine (adrenaline).

Relaxation Response

- After the crisis or argument, the levels of stress hormones decrease, and the various body systems return to normal.
- Negative thoughts about your spouse give way to warm and caring thoughts.
- You are able to make sense of your argument, repair your hurts, and once again feel safe and connected with each other.
- You are relaxed in your relationship and able to enjoy each other.

Constant Stress

- Constant bickering or long, simmering negative thoughts of your spouse put a grey cloud over all your interactions and keeps you in a protective and defensive stance.
- This keeps you in a low-level state of constant stress. Your body is unable to fully experience the relaxation response. You are not able to feel warm, safe, and close to your spouse. This kind of wear, tear, and strain on your body systems can damage certain organs or organ systems.

As I stated earlier, marriage is hard work. You have to be intentional about nurturing and caring for your spouse. It takes thought and effort to find quality, not leftover, time to be with your spouse. And when you are with your spouse, make the most of your connection.

De-stress your life. To have peaceful and meaningful times together, often couples have to begin by de-stressing their life. When my sons were young, a woman once said to me, "For a mother to have time for herself, she often has to double up; sometimes that means making housework your hobby." How true! But that is what couples do every day of their marriage. They double up spending time together while reviewing the kids' schedule. Or they spend unwinding-in-the-evening time going over the finances. But the greatest double-up mistake is when couples use their date night as a time to discuss the decisions and stresses of the home. It is hard to enjoy a date night when you are talking about money, kids, work, a messy house, or a swamped upcoming weekend. I encourage you to de-stress and simplify your life. That might include reducing the amount of outside activities you and your children are involved in. Open your schedules to allow for time to think, relax, and de-stress.

3. Connect with Rituals

A powerful way to build your marriage friendship is to build meaningful rituals together. No, I am not telling you to add any more time-consuming projects to your already filled schedule. Instead, take the everyday routine activities of life and attach to them a meaningful activity. Attach a meaningful interaction with such mundane tasks of life as waking up, saying hello or good-bye, and eating meals. By doing so, you build rituals that are positive, predictable, and easy enough that you both look forward to them.

Waking up, express love for each other. When you wake up, remind yourself: *This is the day the Lord has made, let us rejoice and be glad in it.* Then turn toward your spouse, smile, and say, "Good morning, sweetheart. I am glad I have you." If you wake up before your spouse, pray over him or her before getting out of bed.

Making your bed, share some fun. Flirt and laugh while making the bed together. Don't worry about the way the corners are folded; just enjoy each other. You are alive and you have someone to share life with. Value your husband and let him feel loved.

Getting ready, share your worlds with each other. As you dress and get ready for your day, talk about what you each have on your schedule for the day. Get to know each other's world and take interest in what your spouse is involved in. Gain an image of what your husband faces each time he walks out of the bedroom door and into the world. Keep in mind what times of the day might be stressful for your wife. Remembering your spouse during the day will keep you sensitive and attuned.

Pray at breakfast. Take several minutes to pray for each other at breakfast, holding hands as you do. Bless your wife, encourage your husband, and speak hope into each other's life. The mere ritual of praying for each other is powerful. If your husband doesn't want to participate, keep it simple. Say a simple, nonthreatening but appropriate blessing to your husband: "I pray God gives you wisdom as you put together your project." "I pray God helps you find the right words as you give your presentation."

Say good-bye with a romantic hugfest. Hug and embrace for forty-five seconds. Really! Look into each other's eyes and tell each other you are still in love. Yes, for many couples this will be uncomfortable at first, but keep doing it until it becomes something you automatically do. It is a powerful and soothing ritual. Husbands, realize that for your wife a warm hug will often melt her anger and frustration. Let her lean into your body and feel your strength and let her know that no matter what, everything will work out. What a powerful way to send each other into the world.

Remember each other during the lunch hour. Try to find a time for a mid-day connection. A quick phone call, e-mail, or text message can take ninety seconds to do but can have priceless impact. Don't see this as an intrusion to your day. If you respond with irritation, "What are you calling about now?" your spouse will respond defensively, feel hurt, and not be glad to see you when you arrive home. Checking in says, "I am thinking of you and care for you."

Driving home, check in again. On the way home call your spouse and find out the plans for the evening. Anything needed for the kids or dinner? Have plans changed? Just let each other know you care and want to be involved in the family's evening activities. This can also be a chance to say, "I look forward to seeing you."

Welcome him/her home and celebrate your life together. When you hear your spouse open the front door and say, "Honey, I'm home," put down what you are doing and walk to the front door. Make greeting each other at the end of each day of great importance. You will need to get off the phone, put down the newspaper, click off the Internet, and walk to the front door. Take another forty-five seconds to hug each other, look into each other's eyes, say a kind word, and touch each other's face. Melt each other's stress away. Yes, this probably takes about four minutes, total. It's not much time, but once again, the impact is priceless. What if the kids try to get into the action? Let them know that daddy and mommy are having their hug time, and in four minutes it will be time for the kids. But daddy is excited to see his wife because he cherishes her. And his wife is proud of him and lets him know. This is a powerful ritual to model for your sons and daughters.

Say good night, I am glad I have you! I think the most powerful ritual a couple can have is the ritual of going to bed together. This is the unwinding of the day, reconnecting, catching up on all that is happening in each other's life, and caring enough to listen. Sit together, be together, and enjoy each other. And when you do climb into bed, speak a blessing to each other. Maybe hold each other, scratch each other's back, touch each other's cheek, and say something meaningful to each other. Find something affirming to say, focusing on the positives and strengths of your spouse, such as:

- "You are a great mother to the kids. Thanks for dinner tonight."
- "I appreciate the hard work you do. Thanks for taking the trash out. I am glad you are my husband."

4. Be Intimate Often

So would you like more sex; longer, passionate foreplay; more romantic walks; more deep talks; more laughter and joy? What husband or wife would not? As husband and wife, it is important to carve out a meaningful sex life, one that is filled with warm and caring expressions of love and value. Adding more sex won't lead to fulfilling intimacy, but an emotionally connected marriage will foster a more meaningful sex life.

When Brad and Shannon first came to a Haven of Safety Marriage Intensive, they reflected the struggle of many couples. Their marriage had been filled with unresolved hurts, and both walked through their relationship protected and defensive—not an atmosphere that encourages desire and passion. Over the years, Brad argued for more sex, and Shannon was hardly ever in the mood. "I stopped asking for sex," Brad said. "I was tired of being rejected." "I didn't know what more he wanted from me," Shannon shared. "Brad didn't understand how tired I was at the end of each day, and I just didn't have any desire for sex." Brad added, "I was fighting for more sex, but I realized our relationship needed to change on many levels in order for us to feel close and connected enough for our intimacy to grow."

According to Dr. Catherine Hart Weber, coauthor of the national study on male and female sexuality, couples are faced with a very real dilemma: men emotionally connect through sex and women through meaningful connection. A man is usually willing to have a meaningful conversation after sex and a wife more receptive to sex after a meaningful conversation. So who goes first? Many an argument revolves around just this. And to make matters worse, when a couple is stuck arguing, they are unable to have connecting conversations, and intimacy gets entangled with the hurt and resentment.

God designed intimacy to be a meaningful time for both husband and wife, a time where hearts, bodies, and emotions are intertwined and connected. It is of great importance for you and your spouse to find a sweet rhythm of connecting through sexual intimacy—it is a powerful way of coming close and feeling connected. However, know right from the start that sticking a date night at the end of your week will not turn on the desire switch. The big dates are not the ones that will increase your desire for sex or warm your heart toward your spouse. Rather, the ongoing, gentle turning toward each other is what builds a foundation of romance, fun, and passion into your marriage. Feeling close and connected to your spouse on Saturday night is based on all the humorous, fun, and flirtatious moments you and your spouse had over the course of the week.

Be more aware of the small everyday moments of your week.

Make sure you talk, share, hug, kiss, and emotionally connect every day. I am certain this will change your sex life. Your wife's heart will be a lot more receptive to your sexual advances if you offer her a chance to sit down and talk about her day or if you give her a foot massage when she plops down on the couch next to you to watch television. Have compassion for your wife. If she is swamped with kids, if she is not feeling well, or if you have argued all week, she will probably not be in the mood for intimacy, but she will be in the mood for your love, understanding, and tenderness.

To honor your wife and be a man of integrity before God, keep your sexual energy turned toward your wife. Remember, looking with lust at other women is dangerous. The images you add to the picture show in your mind should involve only your wife. Despite your arguments and the lack of sex in your marriage, choose to be a man of integrity before God, a man who chooses to be pure in both thought and action.

To the wives, arguments and unresolved hurts can often close your heart, making you less receptive to intimacy. Therefore, do your part in resolving the hurts and filling your everyday interactions with warmth and laughter. There is a careful balance between your husband's sexual needs and your own longing to emotionally connect, so help foster a win-win situation.

Both husbands and wives need to be intentional about creating moments that help them feel emotionally connected with each other. Be careful not to let a wedge come between you and your spouse that hinders your ability to connect sexually. Talk about your lack of desire or your hurts. And if you are stuck, get professional advice. You don't have to live with an unfulfilled and frustrating sex life. Both of you need opportunities to turn your sexual energies toward each other.

As a wife, allow yourself to enjoy your intimate times with your husband. If you find your desire is low, start by anticipating your time together by reflecting on the positive things you enjoy and appreciate about your husband and your marriage. Refer to your list in chapter

6. As Dr. Catherine Hart Weber says, this primes your pump for love and desire, which is the greatest aphrodisiac for women. Then fold into your intimacy time an activity that you enjoy. For example, include in foreplay a back massage, hot bath and music, or have your husband rub your hands and feet with sweet-smelling oil. Be creative. What will make you look forward to running upstairs, closing the bedroom door, and spending intimate time with your husband?

Through the course of Brad and Shannon's intensive, Brad began to realize that the key to Shannon's heart and sexual passion was his gentle spirit. Shannon began to realize that her fear and lack of energy to deal with their sexual problems only kept them disconnected, but to be intimate, what she needed was to feel connected. A no-win cycle.

At the end of their marriage intensive, Brad reached for Shannon's hand and kissed it. In a soft tone of voice he said, "I now know what you meant ten years ago."

Perplexed she asked, "What do you mean?"

"I never knew what you meant when you said you wanted us to emotionally connect. I thought I was a good husband, and you should stop hurting me with your anger and be willing to have sex more often."

"I remember those years," Shannon answered. "I was so angry. I felt pushed out and alone. Sex with you was the last thing on my mind."

"I spent most of my time blaming you for being an angry wife. Now I get it," Brad said almost with excitement. "Now I want to be connected to you, to share life on a heart level."

"I also realize how hurtful my ignoring your sexual needs was. But now when you show interest in who I am as a person," Shannon answered, "I want to come closer to you."

When you and your spouse are emotionally connected, something amazing takes place in your marriage relationship. When you know your spouse truly cares for you, respects you, values you, and is connected to you, intimacy becomes more meaningful.

5. Watch for Defining Moments

A defining moment is a fork in the road of your interaction. How you say what you want to say—your attitude, choice of words, body language, tone of voice, and undertone—determines which direction your conversation will go. One road is a positive road that enables you and your spouse to turn toward each other. The other leads to negativity and turning away from each other. These defining moments can, in an instant, move a conversation from positive and connecting to negative and hurtful.

If you think about it, you will realize that you are constantly faced with these moments, especially when you are tired and careless with your words and attitudes and react instinctively in the moment rather than pausing and choosing to be kind, well-mannered, and thoughtful.

Here are some defining moments that can take your interaction in one of two ways:

1. *The start of a conversation.* If you start it negatively and with an irritated or critical tone of voice, it will probably trigger the same from your spouse.

2. *The small requests and responses.* Be aware of how you talk to your spouse in the small things, such as when you are requesting something, irritated about something, in a hurry, or telling your spouse something. Imagine your spouse saying the following phrases with a smile on his or her face and a warm tone of voice. How does it make you want to respond?
   - "Can you move over?"
   - "Excuse me, you are in my way!"
   - "Do you mind—can I finish what I am doing before I help you?"
   - "Are you going to sit there all night or are you going to help me?"

- "Can you please pass me the jam?"
- "Did you finish the last of the milk?"

Now imagine your spouse saying the same phrase with an irritated tone of voice along with rolling of the eyes and exhaling loudly. How does it make you want to respond? Probably a 180-degree difference.

Other ways we can change a defining moment from a negative to a positive:

What you usually say when you are hurt or frustrated:

A less destructive way to say what you are really feeling:

You are so insensitive.	What I need from you is some understanding, maybe a kind and encouraging word.
Oh, be quiet!	Can you stop for a minute? I feel flooded. Can you say what you just said in a different way?
You have got to be kidding me!	Your idea is one option. I was just thinking of another option. Would you be willing to consider it?
Do you always have to complain?	I don't know what to do with your feelings. I do care about you; I don't know what to do or say.
Are you done?	I feel at a loss for words and can't organize my thoughts as quickly as you can. I feel overwhelmed and am running out of energy to continue arguing right now.

We all have defining moments during our interactions with our spouse. These moments, when filled with negativity, have the power to express disrespect, irritation, and entitlement, triggering an argument. When we become more aware of these moments and the powerful choice we have in the midst of them, we change the emotional atmosphere of our marriage relationship.

When you come to a defining moment: Choose to be a safe place for your spouse. Choose to listen more, attempting to look at situations through the lens of your spouse, and be more understanding. Apologize more and be more willing to forgive. Choose to focus on the good in your spouse. Choose to be more playful, adventurous, and loving. Be a more willing partner in sex. Choose to turn to your faith and the power of prayer for courage and peace.

You can decide to wake up each morning and say, "Good morning, sweetheart. This is the day the Lord has made, let us rejoice and be glad in it. I am glad I have you. How can I support and encourage you in your day today?"

> We should love people not only with words and talk, but by our actions and true caring.
>
> —1 John 3:18 (NCV)
>
> When you talk, do not say harmful things, but say what people need—words that will help others become stronger. Then what you say will do good to those who listen to you.
>
> Do not be bitter or angry or mad. Never shout angrily or say things to hurt others. Never do anything evil. Be kind and loving to each other, and forgive each other just as God forgave you in Christ.
>
> —Ephesians 4:29, 31–32 (NCV)

QUESTIONS AND EXERCISES

1. Discuss with your spouse how you can de-stress and simplify your life to make emotional space, time, and energy to invest in your friendship.

2. What are everyday tasks that you can turn into connecting rituals? With your spouse, write out affirming statements you can say when you wake up, leave for work, return home, and go to bed.

3. How can you foster an atmosphere that will help improve your intimacy together? Discuss with your spouse what he/she needs to feel more comfortable with intimacy and eager for sex.

4. Think back over the last week. When did you experience defining moments, where you could have reacted either negatively or positively?

5. When faced with these defining moments or forks in the road when you could be either grumpy, irritable, negative, and critical, or positive, affirming, and well-mannered— how do you typically react? How could you choose a more positive way of responding and interacting with your spouse?

6. How can you better love, respect, and cherish your spouse?

A FINAL NOTE FROM
DR. SHARON MORRIS MAY

I HAVE COME TO REALIZE THAT GOD IS REAL AND FAITHFUL. I have experienced firsthand that nothing has entered my life that has not been sifted through the hands of God, which are nail-scarred hands of mercy and love. Life is not easy, but in the midst of our pain and suffering we always have a choice: to either be destroyed or refined. Hard times have the potential to chip away at our hope and slowly create in us an attitude of resentfulness or helplessness. But life lived in the presence of God truly does make all the difference in the world.

Life is worth living because God is real and He does make a difference. I am able to find the courage to change because of the strength God gives me. Christ goes before me, and in the calm of His wake I find the strength, peace, and encouragement to live life to its fullest.

It is my hope that you will find the path to God and live the abundant life He offers. It is my prayer that you not give up hope. Never give up hope for your marriage, your husband, your wife, or your family.

If you do not know God, I invite you to explore who He is. Read the Bible along with a book that can explain what the Christian life is all about. God does exist, and all that He says in the Bible is true.

God can make a difference in your life. You will never know what difference until you seek Him, know Him, and choose to live in His shelter.

If you once knew God, but have spent the past season of your life lukewarm, distant, and disconnected, I encourage you to seek Him out. Life lived in the shelter of God Most High is a worthwhile life. You know that. Don't waste time; find your way back to God. All you have to do is seek Him, and you will find Him. He promises it.

Jeremiah 29:11–13

Psalm 91

I do not know you. But you will be in my prayers.

—SHARON MORRIS MAY

And I pray that you and all God's holy people will have the power to understand the greatness of Christ's love— how wide and how long and how high and how deep that love is. Christ's love is greater than anyone can ever know, but I pray that you will be able to know that love . . .

—**Ephesians 3:18–19** (NCV)

NOTES

Introduction

1. Emotionally Focused Therapy (EFT) was originated by Dr. Susan Johnson and Dr. Les Greenberg. I was introduced to EFT by Dr. Brent Bradley, a fellow student in graduate school and now a well-respected professor at Wesleyan University, subsequently trained by Dr. Susan Johnson. Haven of Safety Marriage Intensives, based on a Christian view of EFT and attachment theory, aims to help couples make sense of and change their argument cycles by helping them foster emotionally connected relationships. This book is based on my work with couples in the Haven of Safety Marriage Intensives and aims to view couples' arguments through the lens of attachment theory and draws from the steps of change outlined in EFT.

2. Research by Neil Jacobson in his book *Reconcilable Differences*, report given by Mike McManus at WinShape Leaders Retreat 2004, and report given by Susan Johnson at conference in San Diego, 2004.

Chapter One

1. These findings are based on research by John Gottman.

2. "We all show the Lord's glory, and we are being changed to be like him . . ." 2 Corinthians 3:18 (NCV).

Chapter Two

1. John Bowlby, *Attachment and Loss, Volume 1: Attachment* (New York: Basic Books, 1969, 1982), 182.

2. "Then the LORD God took dust from the ground and formed a man from it. He breathed the breath of life into the man's nose, and the man became a living person. Then the LORD God planted a garden. Then the LORD God said, 'It is not good for the man to be alone. I will make a helper who is right for him.' So

a man will leave his father and mother and be united with his wife, and the two will become one body" Genesis 2:7–8, 18, 24 (NCV).

3. Daniel Siegel, *The Developing Mind: How Relationships and the Brain Interact to Shape Who We Are* (New York: Guilford, 1999), 72.

4. Attachment Theory is a theory of love that outlines why we love and hurt the way we do in relationships. Current research has built upon attachment theory to understand how the brain develops in our early relationships and the neurobiology of attachments. A thorough book on understanding how our growing up shapes who we are is *Becoming Attached: Unfolding the Mystery of the Infant-Mother Bond and Its Impact on Later Life* by Robert Karen (New York: Warner, 1994).

5. John Bowlby, *Attachment and Loss: Volume. 2: Separation: Anxiety and Anger* (New York: Basic Books, 1973), 23.

6. John Bowlby says that our most painful emotions are felt when we are forming, maintaining, and breaking our most valued bonds.

7. For further reading, see "The Emotional Dynamics of Disruptions in Attachment Relationships" by R. Kobak in Jude Cassidy and Philip R. Shaver's, *Handbook of Attachment* (New York: Guilford Press, 1999), 33.

ABOUT THE AUTHOR

Sharon (Hart) Morris May, PhD, is the originator of the highly acclaimed Haven of Safety Marriage Relationship Intensives and Conferences at the Hart Institute in Pasadena, California. With a doctorate in marriage and family therapy from Fuller Graduate School of Psychology, Dr. Sharon Morris May is an internationally known expert in emotionally focused therapy. Author of *Safe Haven Marriage*, as well as numerous articles and chapters in books on relationships, she is the contributing editor for *Marriage and Family: A Christian Journal*. Dr. Morris May and her husband, Mike, live in southern California surrounded by their four sons.

Dr. Morris May is available for couple intensives and counselor training and to speak at your couples' conferences, women's conference, churches, and graduate school universities.

She also is available for radio and television interviews

and

Haven of Safety Marriage Intensives and Conferences:

Two- to Four-Day Marriage Intensives

One- to Two-Day Marriage Conferences

For a One-Hour Talk (CD format) for Couples,
Titled *How to Argue So Your Spouse Will Listen,*
Please Order at: www.havenofsafety.com

Couples Workbook and Video Series also Available

Counselor Training Resources Include:
- CD or DVD Training in *Emotionally Focused Couple Therapy Training*
- Training Series for Pastors and Counselors in the Haven of Safety Marriage Intensives Model
- 6-Week Tele-Couples Counseling Training
- Counselor Supervision and Training via Telephone

To Be Added to Our Mailing List
or for Information and a Free Brochure, Contact:
Dr. Sharon Morris May
Haven of Safety Relationships
P. O. Box 80828
San Marino, CA 91118
626-447-6663
argue@havenofsafety.com
www.havenofsafety.com
www.hartinstitute.com